THE CALIFORNIA DIRECTORY OF
FINE WINERIES

EIGHTH EDITION

THE CALIFORNIA DIRECTORY OF
FINE WINERIES

K. REKA BADGER, CHERYL CRABTREE,
AND DANIEL MANGIN, WRITERS

ROBERT HOLMES, PHOTOGRAPHER

TOM SILBERKLEIT, EDITOR AND PUBLISHER

CONTENTS

INTRODUCTION

Whether you are a visitor or a native seeking the ultimate chalice of nectar from the grape, navigating Northern California's wine country can be intimidating. Hundreds of wineries —from glamorous estates to converted barns, from nationally recognized labels to hidden gems— are found throughout Napa, Sonoma, and Mendocino. The challenge is deciding where to go and how to plan a trip. This book will be your indispensable traveling companion.

The sixty-seven wineries in this fully updated eighth edition of *The California Directory of Fine Wineries* are known for producing some of the world's most admired wines. From the moment you walk in the door of these wineries, you will be greeted like a guest and invited to sample at a relaxing, leisurely tempo. Although the quality of the winemaker's art is of paramount importance, the wineries are also notable as tourist destinations. Many boast award-winning contemporary architecture, while others are housed in lovingly preserved historical structures. Some have galleries featuring museum-quality artwork by local and international artists or exhibits focusing on the region's past and the history of winemaking. You will also enjoy taking informative behind-the-scenes tours, exploring inspirational gardens, and participating in celebrated culinary programs. Many wineries require reservations for tastings, and with a bit of advance planning, you also can arrange to take part in a barrel sampling, a blending seminar, or a grape stomping.

As you explore this magnificent region, you'll encounter some of California's most appealing scenery and attractions—mountain ranges, rugged coastline, pastures with majestic oak trees, abundant parkland, renowned spas, and historic towns. Use the information in this book to plan your trip, and be sure to stop along the way and take in the sights. You have my promise that traveling to your destination will be as pleasurable as the wine tasted upon your welcome.

—Tom Silberkleit
Editor and Publisher
Wine House Press
Sonoma, California

THE ETIQUETTE OF WINE TASTING

Most of the wineries profiled in this book offer amenities ranging from lush gardens to art exhibitions, but their main attraction is the tasting room. This is where winery employees get a chance to share their products and knowledge with consumers, in hopes of establishing a lifelong relationship. They are there to please.

Yet, for some visitors, the ritual of tasting fine wines can be intimidating. Perhaps it's because swirling wine and using a spit bucket seem to be unnatural acts. But with a few tips, even a first-time taster can enjoy the experience. After all, the point of tasting is to enhance your knowledge by learning the differences among varieties of wines, styles of winemaking, and appellations.

A list of available wines is usually posted, beginning with whites and ending with the heaviest reds or, if available, dessert wines. Look for the tasting notes, which are typically set out on the counter; refer to them as you taste each wine. A number of wineries charge a tasting fee for four or five wines of your choosing or for a "flight"—most often several preselected wines. In any event, the tasting process is the same.

After you are served, hold the stem of the glass with your thumb and as many fingers as you need to maintain control. Lift the glass up to the light and note the color and intensity of the wine. Good wines tend to be bright, with the color fading near the rim. Next, gently swirl the wine in the glass. Observe how much of the wine adheres to the sides of the glass. If lines—called legs—are visible, the wine is viscous, indicating body or weight as well as a high alcohol content. Now, tip the glass to about a 45-degree angle, take a short sniff, and concentrate on the aromas. Swirl the wine again to aerate it, releasing additional aromas. Take another sniff and see if the "bouquet" reminds you of anything—rose petals, citrus fruit, or a freshly ironed pillowcase, for example—that will help you identify the aroma.

Finally, take a sip and swirl the wine around your tongue, letting your taste buds pick up all the flavors. The wine may remind you of honey or cherries or mint—as with the "nosing," try to make as many associations as you can. Then spit the wine into the bucket on the counter. Afterward, notice how long the flavor stays in your mouth; a long finish is the ideal. If you don't want another taste, just pour the wine remaining in your glass into the bucket and move on. Remember, the more you spit or pour out, the more wines you will enjoy sampling.

The next level of tasting involves food-and-wine pairings. In these sessions, appetizers—or perhaps cheeses, nuts, dried fruit, or charcuterie—are paired with a flight presented in the recommended order of tasting. The server will explain what goes with what and how the flavors of the food and the wine complement each other.

If you still feel self-conscious, practice at home. When you are in a real tasting room, you'll be better able to focus on the wine itself. That's the real payoff, because once you learn what you like and why you like it, you'll be able to recognize wines in a similar vein anywhere in the world.

WHAT IS AN APPELLATION?

Winemakers often showcase the source of their fruit by citing an appellation to describe the area where the grapes were grown. An appellation is a specific region that, in the United States, was traditionally determined by political borders such as state and county lines. Since the institution in 1981 of a system of American Viticultural Areas (AVAs), those borders have been based on climate and geography. Preexisting politically defined appellations were grandfathered into the new system of AVAs, administered these days by the U.S. Alcohol and Tobacco Tax and Trade Bureau (TTB). Using the name of either an appellation or an AVA on a label requires that a certain percentage of the wine in the bottle (75 and 85 percent, respectively) be made from grapes grown within the designation.

AVAs, in contrast to appellations, are defined by such natural features as soil types, prevailing winds, rivers, and mountain ranges. Wineries or other interested parties hoping to create an AVA must submit documented research to the TTB proving that the area's specific attributes distinguish it from the surrounding region. The TTB has the authority to approve or deny the petition.

Winemakers know that identifying the origin of their grapes can lend prestige to a wine, particularly if the AVA or appellation has earned a reputation for quality. It also provides information about what's inside the bottle. For instance, informed consumers know that a Chardonnay from the Napa Valley is apt to differ in both aroma and taste from a Sonoma Coast Chardonnay. When a winery uses grapes from an off-site AVA or appellation to make a particular wine, the label indicates the source of the fruit, not the location of the winery.

The following are the appellations in Napa, Sonoma, and Mendocino, which themselves are part of the larger North Coast appellation.

NAPA

Atlas Peak
Calistoga
Chiles Valley
Coombsville
Diamond Mountain District
Howell Mountain
Los Carneros
Mt. Veeder
Napa Valley
North Coast
Oak Knoll District of
    Napa Valley
Oakville
Rutherford
Spring Mountain District
St. Helena
Stags Leap District
Wild Horse Valley
Yountville

SONOMA

Alexander Valley
Bennett Valley
Chalk Hill
Dry Creek Valley
Fort Ross–Seaview
Fountaingrove District
Green Valley of
    Russian River Valley
Knights Valley
Los Carneros
Moon Mountain District
    Sonoma County
North Coast
Northern Sonoma
Petaluma Gap (pending)
Pine Mountain–Cloverdale Peak
Rockpile
Russian River Valley
Sonoma Coast
Sonoma Mountain
Sonoma Valley
West Sonoma Coast (pending)

MENDOCINO

Anderson Valley
Cole Ranch
Covelo
Dos Rios
Eagle Peak Mendocino County
McDowell Valley
Mendocino
Mendocino Ridge
North Coast
Pine Mountain–Cloverdale Peak
Potter Valley
Redwood Valley
Sanel Valley (pending)
Ukiah Valley (pending)
Yorkville Highlands

MODERN STOPPERS:
CORK, PLASTIC, AND SCREWCAPS

It's an ancient question: What is the best way to close a wine bottle? Since the late 1600s, vintners have largely chosen stoppers made from cork tree bark. These time-tested closures usually provide an effective seal, potentially lasting as long as thirty years or more. At the same time, they are elastic and compressible, which allows for easy extraction. Many wine aficionados associate cork stoppers with a hallowed ritual, using corkscrews or other devices to remove the cork and launch the wine appreciation experience.

Corks, however, are not perfect stoppers. In past years, statistics estimated that nearly 20 percent of wine bottles were damaged by cork taint." This results from natural unnatural chemical compounds sources, for example, pesticides compounds contaminate the chemicals that give the wine a occasionally disintegrate and corks fail by allowing too much  problems, chiefly from "cork airborne fungi meeting up with (pollutants from industrial and wood preservatives). The cork bark and produce other musty odor. Contaminated corks crumble in the bottle. Some oxygen to pass through to the wine. Cork advocates claim that recent research has reduced the risk of cork taint to as little as 1 percent. Any risk at all is unacceptable to some winemakers, who now rely on other types of bottle stoppers.

Screwcaps, once associated with inexpensive, mass-produced wines, have grown increasingly popular in many countries around the world. The caps hold in place a seal liner, designed to allow a microscopic amount of breathability for aging wines over time. And they are easy to remove. More and more wineries are using screwcaps with great success, virtually eliminating the occurrence of damaged wine due to closure problems.

Synthetic (plastic) stoppers also offer a reliable sealing solution. They act in the same manner as corks and are removed from bottles with corkscrews and similar devices. Synthetic corks can provide an excellent seal. However, many are not as flexible as cork, and a highly effective seal can make them difficult to remove from the bottle. Additionally, some lose their elasticity within a few years and are not good candidates for wines meant to age long-term.

Choice of stoppers also involves environmental considerations. The western Mediterranean region contains 6.6 million acres of cork oak tree (*Quercus suber*) forests. Bark from mature trees is harvested in environmentally friendly fashion every nine years, and trees typically live from 150 to 200 years. Cork stoppers are natural, renewable, recyclable, and biodegradable. The forests support wildlife habitats, absorb carbon dioxide from the atmosphere, and sustain local workers. Plastic can be recycled, but it is not made from environmentally friendly material and is not a sustainable product. Screwcaps are recyclable, but the manufacturing process requires much energy usage and releases greenhouses gases into the atmosphere. In recent years, stoppers made with renewable plant-based polymers have shown promise, with one manufacturer claiming a far lower carbon footprint than occurs with screwcaps or cork or plastic stoppers.

As the stopper debate continues to rock the wine world, some wineries are returning to a simple, environmentally friendly solution used for centuries. They sell whole barrels directly to restaurants and tasting rooms, which offer "barrel wines" on tap to customers—no stoppers, bottles, or packaging at all.

The Making of Wine

Most vintners agree that wine is made not in the cellar, but in the vineyard, where sun, soil, climate, altitude, and water—collectively known as *terroir*—influence varietal flavor. Growers select vineyard sites for many reasons, including sun or wind exposure and low fertility, because lean soils often produce the most flavorful fruit. Based on the *terroir*, they plant varietals and clones (also called subvarietals) that will grow best, and then wait three years or longer for the vines to mature before ever picking a grape.

Harvest brings intense activity, as truckloads of ripe grapes roll into the winery, ready to be crushed and destemmed. After crush, white grapes are pressed, and their juice sent to barrels or stainless steel tanks for fermentation, while red grapes are fermented with skins and seeds to provide additional color and flavor. Winemakers introduce commercially grown yeast or sometimes rely on ambient wild yeast to trigger fermentation, a roiling process during which yeast converts grape sugar into alcohol and carbon dioxide. Fermentation stops when the yeast runs out of sugar, which results in a dry wine. Conversely, the winemaker may quickly chill the wine, killing the yeast and leaving behind a little residual sugar for sweetness.

After fermentation, many wines spend from a few months to a year or more in oak barrels where they develop complexity and absorb hints of the toasted interior of the barrel itself. Red wines usually rest in the barrel longer than whites. Most rosés and crisp white wines, such as Riesling, spend little or no time in barrels.

Throughout the process, winemakers taste their young wares, checking for signs of spoilage and imbalance. They analyze samples in a laboratory to determine the chemical makeup of the wine, which helps them to correct potential problems and maintain stability as the wines continue to evolve. Prior to bottling, vintners spend hours tasting wine from tanks and barrels to create optimum combinations for their final blends. Once in the bottle, rosés and light, fruity whites are usually released within a few months. Robust reds remain at the winery for several months to a year or so, which gives them a chance to mature and soften before their release.

To make sparkling wine using the *méthode champenoise*, vintners combine a blended base wine—usually Chardonnay or Pinot Noir fermented without the skins—with sugar and yeast. The mixture goes into heavy glass bottles, where a secondary fermentation takes place, giving the wine its signature bubbles. The wine ages for a year or more, and then dead yeast cells are removed in a process called disgorging. A little wine, called the *dosage* (pronounced doh-sahj), often mixed with sugar syrup to balance out the acidity, is added back to the bottle, and a natural cork is wired in place.

Wine lovers often buy several bottles of a favorite vintage and store them in a cellar or cool closet. That way, they can open a bottle every year or so, and enjoy the subtle flavor shifts as the wine continues to mature over time.

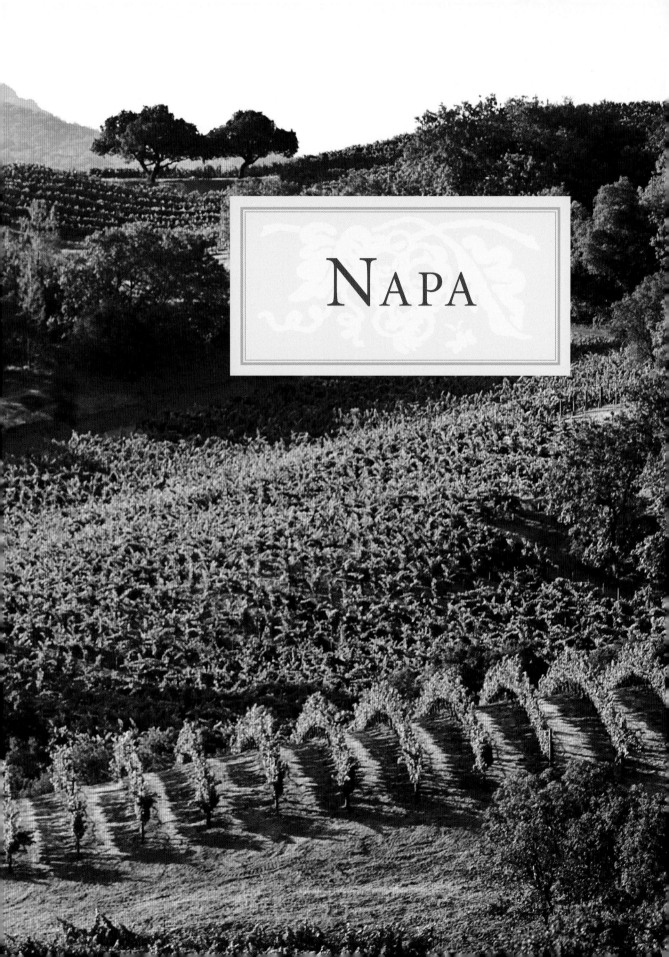

NAPA

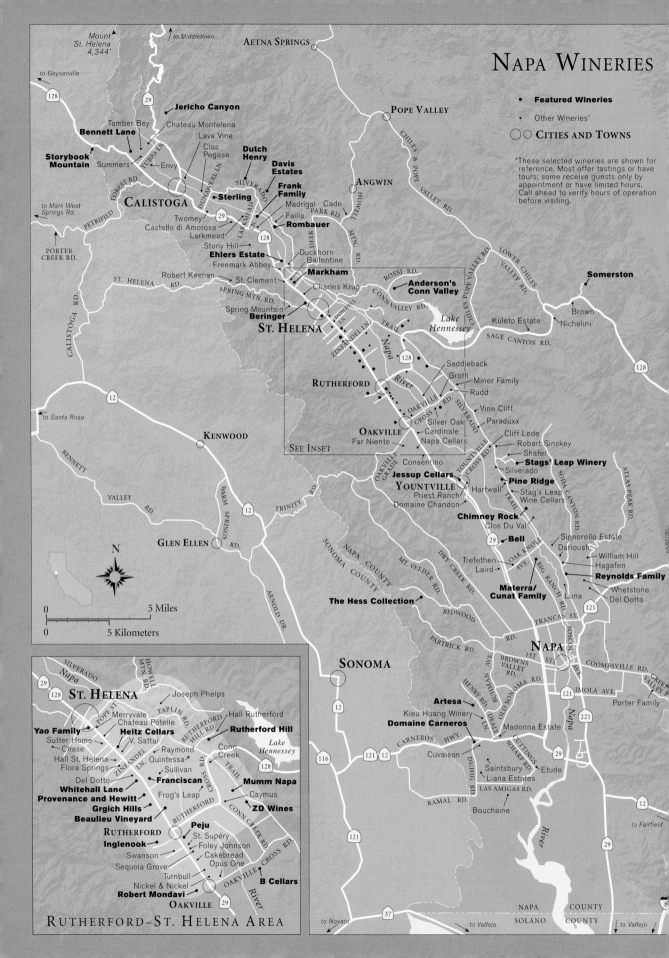

NAPA WINERIES

- • Featured Wineries
- • Other Wineries*
- ◯◯ CITIES AND TOWNS

*These selected wineries are shown for reference. Most offer tastings or have tours; some receive guests only by appointment or have limited hours. Call ahead to verify hours of operation before visiting.

Mount St. Helena 4,344'

to Middletown

AETNA SPRINGS

to Geyserville

128

POPE VALLEY

Jericho Canyon

Tamber Bey
Chateau Montelena
Lava Vine
Clos Pegase
Envy

Bennett Lane

29

Storybook Mountain
Summers

CALISTOGA

to Mark West Springs Rd.

to Santa Rosa

Dutch Henry
Davis Estates
Frank Family
Sterling
Madrigal
Cade
Failla
Rombauer

ANGWIN

Twomey
Castello di Amorosa
Larkmead
Stony Hill
Ehlers Estate
Freemark Abbey
Robert Keenan
St. Clement
Markham
Charles Krug

Anderson's Conn Valley

Somerston

Brown
Nichelini

Kuleto Estate

Lake Hennessey

Beringer
Spring Mountain
ST. HELENA

128

Saddleback
Groth
Miner Family
Rudd

RUTHERFORD

Napa River

Vine Cliff
Paraduxx

Cliff Lede
Robert Sinskey
Shafer

Stags' Leap Winery

KENWOOD

Silver Oak
Cardinale
Napa Cellars
Far Niente

OAKVILLE

Consentino

Jessup Cellars

YOUNTVILLE

Silverado

Pine Ridge

Hartwell
Stag's Leap Wine Cellars

Priest Ranch
Domaine Chandon

Chimney Rock
Clos Du Val

12

GLEN ELLEN

29
Bell

Signorello Estate
Darioush

Trefethen
Laird

William Hill
Hagafen

Reynolds Family

Whetstone
Del Duca

Materra/
Cunat Family

Luna

The Hess Collection

SONOMA

NAPA

Partrick Rd.

Redwood

Artesa
Kieu Hoang Winery
Domaine Carneros

Porter Family

Madonna Estate

Cuvaison

Saintsbury
Liana Estates
Etude

Bouchaine

37

to Novato

to Vallejo

NAPA COUNTY
SOLANO COUNTY

to Vallejo

to Fairfield

RUTHERFORD–ST. HELENA AREA

St. Helena
Joseph Phelps
Merryvale
Chateau Potelle
Hall Rutherford
Rutherford Hill
Heitz Cellars
V. Sattui

Yao Family
Sutter Home
Chase
Hall St. Helena
Flora Springs

Raymond
Quintessa
Sullivan

Lake Hennessey

Del Duca
Franciscan

Whitehall Lane
Provenance and Hewitt
Grgich Hills
Beaulieu Vineyard

Frog's Leap

Mumm Napa
Caymus
ZD Wines

RUTHERFORD
Inglenook

Peju
St. Supéry
Foley Johnson
Cakebread
Opus One

Swanson
Sequoia Grove
Turnbull
Nickel & Nickel
Robert Mondavi

B Cellars

OAKVILLE

29

The Napa Valley, jam-packed with hundreds of premium wineries and thousands of acres of coveted vineyards, has earned its position as the country's number one winemaking region. From its southern tip at San Pablo Bay, about an hour's drive from San Francisco, this picture-perfect patchwork of agriculture extends thirty miles north to the dramatic Palisades that tower above Calistoga. The narrow, scenic valley is defined on the east by a series of  hills known as the Vaca Range and on the west by the rugged peaks of the Mayacamas Mountains, including the steep forested slopes of Mount Veeder.

St. Helena, where upscale stores and chic boutiques line the historic Main Street, is the jewel in the region's crown. At the southern end of the valley, the city of Napa has experienced a boom in recent years, with a plethora of restaurants and attractions such as the vibrant Oxbow Public Market. The mostly two-lane Highway 29 links these and smaller towns that welcome visitors with a variety of spas, restaurants, and bed-and-breakfast inns.

For an unforgettable impression, book a hot-air balloon ride or simply drive up the winding Oakville Grade and pull over at the top for a view worthy of a magazine cover.

ANDERSON'S CONN VALLEY VINEYARDS

Less than a ten-minute drive from bustling downtown St. Helena, Anderson's Conn Valley Vineyards occupies a niche in a valley within a valley. The location is so remote that most drivers along Conn Valley Road aren't even aware the winery exists. Out here, you could hear a pin drop, except during the busy harvest season that begins in late summer.

Anderson's Conn Valley Vineyards was founded in 1983 by Todd Anderson and his parents, Gus and Phyllis. Gus Anderson spearheaded the lengthy search for vineyard property in Napa Valley. He had the advantage of realizing Napa's tremendous potential before the region became widely known (in the wake of the famous 1976 Paris tasting that put Napa on the world wine map) and before land in wine country became prohibitively expensive.

Joseph Heitz and Joseph Phelps had already established wineries in the neighborhood by the time the Andersons found their dream site, forty acres in the eastern part of the St. Helena American Viticultural Area near the base of Howell Mountain. Unfortunately, the acreage was not for sale; it would take fifteen months of negotiations to secure the property.

Then the real work of establishing a winery operation began, and for the most part, it has all been done by the Andersons. Todd Anderson left his profession as a geophysicist to pound posts, hammer nails, and install twenty-six and a half acres of prime vineyards. That was just the beginning. While the vines matured, the Andersons created a fifteen-acre-foot reservoir and built the winery, the residence, and a modest cave system.

The family did hire professionals with the necessary heavy-duty equipment to expand the caves by 8,000 square feet. Completed in 2001, the 9,000-square-foot caves feature a warren of narrow pathways beneath the hillside. Deep in the caverns, one wall has been pushed out to make way for tables and chairs where visitors can sample the wines. In clement weather, tastings are often held on the far side of the caves, with seating beneath market umbrellas at an inviting arrangement of tables that overlook the reservoir.

The highly educational tastings are conducted by one of the knowledgeable Anderson's Conn staff members and frequently by owner Todd Anderson. A great advantage to touring a family winery is the chance to get to know the people behind the wines and to linger long enough to ask questions that might never get answered during a large group tour at one of Napa's big and better-known wineries located along either Highway 29 or the Silverado Trail.

ANDERSON'S CONN VALLEY VINEYARDS
680 Rossi Rd.
St. Helena, CA 94574
707-963-8600
800-946-3497
info@connvalleyvineyards.com
connvalleyvineyards.com

OWNERS: Anderson family.

LOCATION: 3.3 miles east of Silverado Trail via Howell Mountain Rd. and Conn Valley Rd.

APPELLATION: Napa Valley.

HOURS: 9 A.M.–5 P.M. Monday–Friday; 10 A.M.–2 P.M. Saturday–Sunday.

TASTINGS: By appointment.

TOURS: By appointment.

THE WINES: Cabernet Franc, Cabernet Sauvignon, Chardonnay, Merlot, Pinot Noir, Sauvignon Blanc.

SPECIALTIES: Cabernet Sauvignon, Bordeaux blends.

WINEMAKERS: Todd Anderson, Robert Hunt.

ANNUAL PRODUCTION: 6,500 cases.

OF SPECIAL NOTE: Reserve cave tasting ($65) and private tasting with food pairing hosted by winemaker ($250).

NEARBY ATTRACTIONS: Bothe-Napa State Park (hiking, picnicking, horseback riding, swimming); Robert Louis Stevenson Museum (author memorabilia).

ARTESA VINEYARDS & WINERY

ARTESA VINEYARDS & WINERY
1345 Henry Rd.
Napa, CA 94559
707-224-1668
info@artesawinery.com
artesawinery.com

OWNERS: Codorníu
Raventós family.

LOCATION: 6 miles south-west of downtown Napa, off Old Sonoma Rd.

APPELLATIONS: Los Carneros, Napa Valley.

HOURS: 10 A.M.–5 P.M. daily (last full tasting at 4:30 P.M.).

TASTINGS: $25 for 5 reserve and limited-release wines. Food-and-wine pairings daily (reservations required).

TOURS: 11 A.M. and 2 P.M. daily.

THE WINES: Albariño, Cabernet Sauvignon, Chardonnay, Pinot Noir, Rosé of Pinot Noir, Tempranillo, single-vineyard designates.

SPECIALTIES: Codorníu Napa Grand Reserve sparkling wine, estate-grown Char-donnay and Pinot Noir.

WINEMAKER: Ana Diogo-Draper.

ANNUAL PRODUCTION: 50,000 cases.

OF SPECIAL NOTE: Codorníu Raventós family's wine-making history in Spain dates back to 1551. Under-ground aging cellar cooled naturally by surrounding earth. Many works by artist-in-residence Gordon Huether on exhibit. Cheese and charcuterie plates available. Many reserve and limited-release wines avail-able only in tasting room.

NEARBY ATTRACTION: di Rosa (indoor and out-door exhibits of works by contemporary Bay Area artists).

In 1988 Codorníu Raventós, a Spanish producer known for Cava sparkling wines, commissioned the Barcelona-based architect Domingo Triay to design a hilltop winery on its 350-acre Napa Valley Carneros estate. The winery is submerged discreetly into the hillside behind three bermlike terraces, and its broad entry plaza is reached via a grand three-tiered concrete staircase edged by slender waterfalls.

Jackrabbits, quail, and other creatures often dart across Artesa's driveway as it gently switchbacks past open grassland and rows of Pinot Noir and Chardonnay, to the parking area. Here, atop the lowest terrace, a circular fountain edged by six spikelike, seven-foot-tall aluminum-composite sculptures by Artesa's artist in residence, Gordon Huether

of Napa, hints at the splendor to come. At the top landing of the staircase, a long, narrow oval pool with another fountain—metal columns spaced wide apart and set at dramatic forty-five-degree angles—gives way to a grassy expanse. Farther west along the walk-way is the winery, its mostly grass-covered exterior punc-tuated by the tasting room's entrance and panels of tinted glass that form an inverted pyramid.

First-time visitors often find themselves so awestruck by the architecture and the south-facing views—on clear days extending south past the di Rosa art preserve and San Pablo Bay all the way to San Francisco—that a few minutes pass before their eyes drift east and north to equally captivating views of vineyards, grazing land, and the Vaca Range. Inside the winery, a concierge escorts guests to tastings at one of several bars or tables in the gallerylike indoor space, at an open-air interior courtyard, or on an outdoor terrace facing south. All the spaces invite lingering over a lineup of fine wines built around Napa Valley Chardonnays and Pinot Noirs that also includes Cabernet Sauvignons and two wines from Spanish varietals: Albariño and Tempranillo, a stylishly earthy red.

Artesa means "handcrafted" in Catalan, and the hands crafting Artesa's wines belong to Ana Diogo-Draper. Born and raised in Portugal, she moved to California in 2005 and joined Artesa in 2013. The Artesa style emphasizes holding true to a varietal's characteristics and expressing the geology and climate of the vineyards where the grapes are grown. Artesa Pinot Noirs taste like classic Pinots, and among the pleasures of a tasting here is experiencing the flavor variations depending on the vineyards the grapes come from. Reflecting Artesa's commitment to responsible land manage-ment, those vineyards are farmed using certified sustainable practices.

B CELLARS VINEYARDS AND WINERY

The lead partners of B Cellars hail from the world of luxury resorts and retail, so it should come as no surprise that guests rave about the winery's polished hospitality and first-class wines and cuisine. B Cellars, which opened in 2003 in Calistoga and in 2014 moved to a twelve-acre former horse ranch in Oakville, achieved quick recognition for winemaker Kirk Venge's fruit-forward blends and single-vineyard Cabernets made with grapes from prestigious Napa Valley sources. To emphasize the wines' food-friendly qualities, all visits revolve around intricate small bites prepared in an open-hearth kitchen in the Hospitality House.

In designing the tasting space winery's architects strove for coated with a faux rust pigment, the bucolic setting. Hospitality clerestory peak ensure an airy feel on sunny afternoons, the sleek

and production buildings, the simplicity. Clad in corrugated steel the structures echo and blend into House's large windows and on even the most subdued day; interior positively glows.

The two main tasting options, Garden Pairing, take about 90 beginning with a tour of the and aging caves. Upon returning the Oakville Trek and the Chef's and 120 minutes respectively, each culinary garden, production facility, to Hospitality House, guests are seated and served separately. A recent winter menu paired flatbread, caramelized onions, pear, and goat cheese with five wines, starting with a white blend (Chardonnay, Sauvignon Blanc, and Viognier). Each wine's components accentuated different aspects of the well-chosen ingredients and vice versa. A similarly successful summer coupling involved a critically acclaimed Cabernet Sauvignon and a chocolate espresso–rubbed New York strip steak and accompanying blackberry bordelaise sauce.

Among the most sought-after B Cellars wines are single-vineyard Cabernets from Missouri Hopper, To Kalon, Georges III, Dr. Crane, and others from Andy Beckstoffer's Heritage Vineyards, arguably the Napa Valley's most historically significant vineyard properties. The prized Beckstoffer reserve wines are poured in the private Beckstoffer Heritage room inside the aging caves.

The Beckstoffer and B Cellars relationship is a tribute to the reputation of Venge, whose early wine knowledge comes from his winemaking father, Nils, himself a local legend for his Saddleback Cellars Cabernets. The younger Venge pushes the envelope regarding ripeness and fruitiness, particularly in nontraditional combinations such as B Cellars' Blend 24, comprised of Cabernet, Sangiovese, and Petite Sirah. As with the B Cellars food, Venge strikes just the right balance between opulence and approachability.

B CELLARS VINEYARDS AND WINERY
703 Oakville Cross Rd.
Oakville, CA 94562
707-709-8787
info@bcellars.com
bcellars.com

OWNERS: Duffy Keys and Jim Borsack.

LOCATION: 14 miles north of Napa, 8 miles south of St. Helena, off the Silverado Trail or Hwy 29.

APPELLATIONS: Atlas Peak, Calistoga, Oakville, Rutherford, St. Helena.

HOURS: 10 A.M.–5 P.M. daily, by appointment.

TASTINGS: Oakville Trek, $60 for 5 wines. Chef's Garden Pairing, $135 for 5 wines. Both include food pairings, cave and property tour, and barrel tasting.

TOURS: Included with tastings.

THE WINES: Cabernet Sauvignon, Chardonnay, Merlot, Petit Verdot, Petite Sirah, Pinot Noir, Sangiovese, Sauvignon Blanc, Syrah, Viognier, Zinfandel.

SPECIALTIES: Blended wines, single-vineyard Beckstoffer Collection Cabernet Sauvignon.

WINEMAKER: Kirk Venge.

ANNUAL PRODUCTION: 7,500 cases.

OF SPECIAL NOTE: First new winery on the Oakville Cross Road in nearly two decades. Lifelike painted bronze figurative sculptures by J. Seward Johnson on grounds.

NEARBY ATTRACTION: Napa Valley Museum (winemaking displays, art exhibits).

BEAULIEU VINEYARD

BEAULIEU VINEYARD
1960 St. Helena Hwy.
Rutherford, CA 94573
800-264-6918, ext. 5233
707-967-5233
visitingbv@bvwines.com
bvwines.com

OWNER: Treasury Wine Estates.

LOCATION: About 3 miles south of St. Helena.

APPELLATION: Rutherford.

HOURS: 10 A.M.–5 P.M. daily.

TASTINGS: Maestro Tasting, $20 for choice of 4 small lot–winery selections. Reserve Tasting, $40 for current vintage of reserve wines including Georges de Latour and Tapestry. Retrospective Reserve Tasting, $60 for flight of 4 older vintage Cabernet Sauvignons.

TOURS: Historic Tour and Barrel Tasting ($35) includes tour of the 1885 winery and BV museum; reservations required.

THE WINES: Cabernet Sauvignon, Chardonnay, Merlot, Sauvignon Blanc.

SPECIALTIES: Rutherford Cabernet Sauvignon, Georges de Latour Private Reserve Cabernet Sauvignon.

WINEMAKER: Jeffrey Stambor.

ANNUAL PRODUCTION: Unavailable.

OF SPECIAL NOTE: Reserve Tasting and Retrospective Tasting held on patio, weather permitting. 13 small-lot wines available only in tasting room. Clone (Cabernet Sauvignon) and Reserve Tapestry (Bordeaux blends) available in the Reserve Room.

NEARBY ATTRACTION: Culinary Institute of America at Greystone (cooking demonstrations).

French immigrant and winemaker Georges de Latour and his wife, Fernande, bought their first Rutherford ranch in 1900. "Beau lieu!" Fernande declared when she saw the ranch, deeming it a "beautiful place." Thus, Beaulieu Vineyard, also known simply as BV, was named. Among the first to recognize Rutherford's potential for yielding stellar Cabernet Sauvignon, Georges de Latour was determined to craft wine to rival the French. By 1909 he had expanded his vineyard and established a nursery for cultivating phylloxera-resistant rootstock. For a time, the nursery supplied a half-million grafted vines annually to California vineyards.

In 1938 de Latour hired André Tchelistcheff, who declared Sauvignon worthy of flagship he introduced a number of practices controlling heat during ferment- delicate fruit flavors, and barrel aging oak barrels for the addition of result, BV's Private Reserve became continues to rank among the region's fabled, Russian-born enologist the 1936 Private Reserve Cabernet status. With de Latour's blessing, now considered standard, including ation to keep wines cool and protect in French, rather than American, more nuanced components. As a Napa Valley's first "Cult Cab" and most widely collected wines.

Housed in a Boston ivy–clad complex built in three different centuries, the gray stone and concrete winery faces the visitor center across a parking lot studded with sycamores and oaks. Guests follow a path edged with manicured boxwood and roses to reach the center, a two-story, hexagonal building with stone exterior. Upon entering, they are immediately handed a complimentary glass of wine in homage to Mrs. de Latour's peerless hospitality. Natural light spills from above, bathing the redwood interior. A curved staircase leads down an open well to the Club Room, where visitors who reserve ahead can enjoy a seated tasting.

A few steps from the visitor center is the Reserve Room, dedicated to the winery's flagship Georges de Latour Private Reserve Cabernet Sauvignon. At a softly lit marble-topped bar, visitors can taste winery exclusives and library wines, or purchase vintages of the Private Reserve going back to 1970. Fieldstone walls mimic those of BV's core winery, built in 1885. In a cozy side room, a glass-topped table displays bottles representing singular moments in the winery's history, including a release of Pure Altar Wine vinified during Prohibition. A brilliant businessman, de Latour prospered despite grape shortages, insect infestations, and Prohibition. More than a century later, Beaulieu Vineyard reigns as a leader in the production of acclaimed Cabernet Sauvignon and is among the longest continually operating wineries in Napa Valley.

BELL WINE CELLARS

Situated only a mile south of downtown Yountville but at the end of a long, quiet access road that makes it feel off the beaten path, Bell Wine Cellars was founded by Anthony Bell, known for his Old World–style Cabernet Sauvignons and research into Cabernet clones. Bell grew up on a wine estate in his native South Africa owned by his father's employer, a major spirits and wine distributor, and by his late teens had become passionate about winemaking. To further his son's wine education, Bell's father arranged for him to work first at a winery that the distributor owned in Spain's sherry district and later at Château Loudenne, a major Bordeaux producer.

After graduating with a master's degree in enology from the University of California, Davis, Bell landed a job in 1979 as assistant winemaker and viticulturist at Napa Valley's Beaulieu Vineyard. While at Beaulieu, Bell brought together grape growers and winemakers, a novel idea at the time, to discuss ways to elevate wine quality. Bell also drew the boundaries for the Carneros appellation and was involved in establishing the Oakville and Rutherford appellations. Bell's duties as Beaulieu's viticulturist led to his participation in a fascinating experiment tracking fourteen types of Cabernet Sauvignon clones to see which produced the best wines. Each year for nearly a decade, grapes were grown and wines were made and tasted blindly. The wine that most often scored the highest was from Clone 6, a Cabernet type long in disuse that a UC Davis researcher had traced to an abandoned vineyard in California's Gold Country.

Bell left Beaulieu in the early 1990s to form the partnership that evolved into the current winery. Not surprisingly, his Clone 6 Rutherford Cabernet Sauvignon is the flagship offering. The winery makes many other Cabernets, representing a single clone or vineyard, as well as proprietary blends. Among the several other varietals are Chardonnay and Merlot produced from estate-grown grapes. Bell credits his experiences in Europe, particularly Bordeaux, with influencing the restrained winemaking style for all his wines, which favor elegance and balance over bravado.

Though Bell has impressive winemaking credentials, a visit to his winery is a casual affair. Current-release tastings take place amid stainless steel tanks holding Sauvignon Blanc and other white wines and, if things get crowded, near oak barrels filled with Cabernet and other reds. Grape to Glass Tours begin where Bell first learned his craft — in the vineyards — for a brief discussion of how grapes grow. After visits to the tanks and barrels, tours conclude with wine-and-cheese pairings. For those intrigued by Bell's clonal investigations, there's a premium Cabernet-only tasting.

BELL WINE CELLARS
6200 Washington St.
Yountville, CA 94599
707-944-1673
info@bellwine.com
bellwine.com

OWNERS: Anthony A. Bell in partnership with the Spanos and Berberian families.

LOCATION: 1 mile south of downtown Yountville.

APPELLATIONS: Yountville, St. Helena, Oakville, Rutherford, Atlas Peak, Coombsville, Mt. Veeder, Calistoga, Napa Valley.

HOURS: 10 A.M.–4 P.M. daily, by appointment.

TASTINGS: $20 for 4 or 5 current-release wines; $50 for 4 or 5 reserve wines. By appointment.

TOURS: 10:30 A.M., 1 P.M., 3 P.M., by appointment.

THE WINES: Cabernet Sauvignon, Chardonnay, Merlot, Sauvignon Blanc, Syrah.

SPECIALTY: Cabernet Sauvignons from Napa, many focusing on a single appellation, vineyard, or clone.

WINEMAKER: Anthony A. Bell.

ANNUAL PRODUCTION: 12,000–14,000 cases.

OF SPECIAL NOTE: Patio tasting area with views of estate Chardonnay and Merlot grapes and beyond them the Mayacamas Mountains. Most wines available only in tasting room.

NEARBY ATTRACTION: Napa Valley Museum (winemaking displays, art exhibits).

BENNETT LANE WINERY

BENNETT LANE WINERY
3340 Hwy. 128
Calistoga, CA 94515
877-629-6272
info@bennettlane.com
bennettlane.com

OWNERS: Randy and
Lisa Lynch.

LOCATION: About 2 miles
north of Calistoga.

APPELLATION: Napa Valley.

HOURS: 10 A.M.–5:30 P.M.
daily.

TASTINGS: $20 for 4 wines;
$35 for seated tasting;
$45 for reserve flight.

TOURS: Daily, by
appointment.

THE WINES: Cabernet
Sauvignon, Chardonnay,
Maximus (red blend),
White Maximus
(white blend).

SPECIALTIES: Cabernet
Sauvignon, Maximus.

WINEMAKER: Rob Hunter.

ANNUAL PRODUCTION:
12,000 cases.

OF SPECIAL NOTE: Varietals
Fruit Flavor Custom
Blend Experience, by
appointment ($225 per
person) and including a
tour and tasting of current
releases with cheese
pairing, allows visitors
to create and bottle their
own wine. Annual events
include Cabernet Release
Weekend (February).
Reserve Chardonnay and
Syrah available only in
tasting room.

NEARBY ATTRACTIONS:
Old Faithful Geyser of
California; Robert Louis
Stevenson State Park
(hiking).

Far from the din and traffic of central Napa Valley, Bennett Lane Winery lures adventuresome Cabernet Sauvignon lovers to the northernmost wedge of the valley, where the Vaca Range meets the Mayacamas Mountains. This sequestered setting just north of the town of Calistoga features dramatic views of Mount St. Helena and the Palisades, which provide an ideal backdrop for Bennett Lane's handcrafted, small-lot wines. Bennett Lane's signature wine is named Maximus, after the second-century Roman emperor Magnus Maximus, a noted vinophile of his day. The exact percentages of varietals that go into the Maximus wines vary somewhat from vintage to vintage. The Maximus Red Feasting Wine is a unique blend, made primarily from Cabernet Sauvignon, with the addition of 20 percent or so Merlot, as well as a small amount of Syrah and, sometimes, Petit Verdot. At Bennett Lane, blending is the name of the game, and tasters eager to learn more about this elusive art are invited to take part in a special program whereby they taste and combine a selection of varietals to create their own Maximus blend.

Visitors to the Mediterranean-style winery are welcomed into a tasting room painted in warm tones of brown and Tuscan gold. Enhancements added during a 2012 remodel include upholstered armchairs for relaxing and a Brazilian granite tasting bar. In order to provide a tasting experience that is enjoyable and educational, as well as interactive, iPads have been mounted along the bar. Here visitors can access a dynamic application that describes Bennett Lane wines and their source vineyards. The app also delivers the latest reviews, detailed tasting notes, and tempting recipes to pair with the wines. The iPads make it easy for tasters to share their wine discoveries with friends via social media, or enter and e-mail their tasting notes to fellow wine lovers.

Owners Randy and Lisa Lynch were relative newcomers to the world of wine in 2003, when they purchased what had once been a custom crush facility. Originally, they had been looking for a second home with vineyard land, and soon after purchasing a residence in Calistoga, they bought the Bennett Lane property. The Lynches were encouraged by critical praise for their wines, whose fruit now comes from highly acclaimed sources in Napa Valley. These vineyards are dotted throughout the valley, from Yountville in the south to Randy Lynch's vineyard in Calistoga in the north. Lynch's goal is to create wines that are both approachable and complex, what he calls "the best of both worlds, meaning you can drink them today, but they are structured enough to cellar for several years."

Beringer Vineyards

With its 1883 Rhine House and hand-carved aging tunnels, Beringer Vineyards is steeped in history like few other California wineries. Established in 1876, at the dawn of California wine, it is the only winery from that founding era that has never missed a vintage. Today, Beringer is widely recognized for combining established traditions with modern elegance.

It was German know-how and the vision that the Napa Valley could produce wines as fine as those from Europe that set the Beringer brothers on the path to glory. Jacob and Frederick Beringer emigrated from Mainz, Germany, to the United States in the 1860s. Jacob, having worked in cellars in Germany, was intrigued when he heard that the California climate was ideal for growing the varietal grapes that flourished in Europe's winemaking regions. Leaving Frederick in New York, he traveled west in 1870 to discover that Napa Valley's rocky, well-drained soils were similar to those in his native Rhine Valley. Five years later, he bought land with Frederick and began excavating the hillsides to create tunnels for aging his wines. During the building of the caves and winery, Jacob lived in an 1848 farmhouse that today is known as the Hudson House. The meticulously restored and expanded structure now serves as Beringer Vineyards' Culinary Arts Center.

The star attraction on the lavishly landscaped grounds is unquestionably the seventeen-room Rhine House, which Frederick modeled after his ancestral home in Germany. The redwood, brick, and stucco mansion is painted in the original Tudor color scheme of earth tones, and slate covers the gabled roof and exterior. The interior of the Rhine House is graced with extraordinary gems of craftsmanship, such as Belgian art nouveau–style stained-glass windows.

Beringer Vineyards was the first winery in Napa Valley to give public tours and continues the tradition with two signature tours, each covering the winery and its fascinating history. An introductory tour takes visitors to the cellars and hand-dug aging tunnels in the Old Stone Winery, where they enjoy wine tasting. A longer, more in-depth tour, the Taste of Beringer, includes a brief tour of the property and demonstration vineyard, followed by a seated tasting in the historic Rhine House. Guests explore the art of wine-and-food pairing by sampling a flight of reserve wines served with seasonal treats prepared by the winery's culinary team.

BERINGER VINEYARDS
2000 Main St.
St. Helena, CA 94574
707-257-5771
beringer.com

OWNER: Treasury Wine Estates.

LOCATION: On Hwy. 29 about .5 mile north of St. Helena.

APPELLATION: Napa Valley.

HOURS: 10 A.M.–5:30 P.M. daily.

TASTINGS AND TOURS: Various options are available. Check beringer.com for information and reservations.

THE WINES: Cabernet Sauvignon, Chardonnay, Merlot, red blends.

SPECIALTIES: Private Reserve Cabernet Sauvignon, single-vineyard Cabernet Sauvignon, Private Reserve Chardonnay.

WINEMAKER: Mark Beringer.

ANNUAL PRODUCTION: Unavailable.

OF SPECIAL NOTE: Tours include visit to barrel storage caves hand-chiseled in late 1800s.

NEARBY ATTRACTIONS: Bothe-Napa State Park (hiking, picnicking, horseback riding, swimming); Robert Louis Stevenson Museum (author memorabilia).

CHIMNEY ROCK WINERY

CHIMNEY ROCK WINERY
5350 Silverado Trail
Napa, CA 94558
800-257-2641
707-257-2641
info@chimneyrock.com
chimneyrock.com

OWNERS: Terlato family.

LOCATION: 3 miles southeast
of downtown Yountville.

APPELLATION: Stags Leap
District.

HOURS: 10 A.M.–5 P.M. daily.

TASTINGS: By appointment,
starting at $50.

TOURS: Estate Tour and
Barrel Tasting, Vertical
Tasting, and Vineyard
Odyssey Tour and Tasting.
By appointment.

THE WINES: Cabernet Franc,
Cabernet Sauvignon,
Merlot, Sauvignon Blanc,
Sauvignon Gris.

SPECIALTIES: 100 percent
estate-grown single-
vineyard Stags Leap District
Cabernet Sauvignons,
Elevage (red Bordeaux
blend), Elevage Blanc
(white Bordeaux blend).

WINEMAKER:
Elizabeth Vianna.

ANNUAL PRODUCTION:
25,000 cases.

OF SPECIAL NOTE: Rotating
display of artworks. Annual
Vineyard to Vintner event
(April) by Stags Leap
District winegrowers.
Winery is pet-friendly.

NEARBY ATTRACTION: Napa
Valley Museum (winemak-
ing displays, art exhibits).

A quarter mile past the elegant wrought iron gates of Chimney Rock Winery, the broad face of the winery gleams beyond converging rows of meticulously farmed Cabernet Sauvignon vines. Whitewashed walls, arched doorways, and soaring gables define and distinguish the eye-catching architecture. Marking the eastern border of the Stags Leap District, the oak-studded Vaca Range is a dramatic backdrop for the winery and harbors the volcanic formation that gave the winery its name.

In 1980 Sheldon "Hack" Wilson, after multiple business successes, turned his talents and resources to making great wines. He, along with his wife, Stella, bought a pristine 185-acre property just south of Yountville and promptly planted 74 acres of Cabernet Sauvignon. By 1990 the couple had completed the tasting room and adjacent winery in the Cape Dutch style of Stella's native South Africa. For the winery's facade, the Wilsons commissioned a decorative frieze that depicts Ganymede — cupbearer to the mythical gods of ancient Greece — which gives the building a timeless, old-world feel. An avid gardener and horticulturist, Stella designed and planted elaborate beds surrounding both their home and the winery. The abundant gardens continue to flourish today.

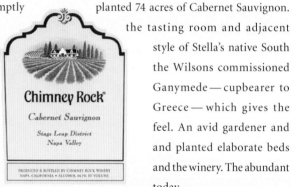

In 2000 the Wilsons partnered with the Terlato family, whose participation in the wine industry had spanned more than fifty years and eleven wine-producing countries. Under the care and guidance of Tony, Bill, and John Terlato, an additional 60 acres were planted to Cabernet Sauvignon, and a new state-of-the-art winery facility was built. After Hack Wilson's death, the Terlato family assumed full ownership of the winery, a gem that includes 119 acres of vineyards devoted almost entirely to the winery's signature Cabernet Sauvignon and other Bordeaux varietals. Over the past decade, the Terlato family has carried the winery and its legacy forward by continuing to produce handcrafted, small-production, single-vineyard wines.

From behind the stately wine bar, staffers warmly greet guests. Just outside the tasting room, a patio with tables and lounge furniture arranged under a wisteria-draped arbor makes a perfect setting to relax with a glass of wine. From this vantage point, visitors can admire Ganymede, the gardens, and, beyond the old winery, the Stags Leap Palisades. To the east is the V-shaped formation where an indigenous Wappo hunter once reported seeing a legendary stag make a diversionary leap to save its herd from flying arrows.

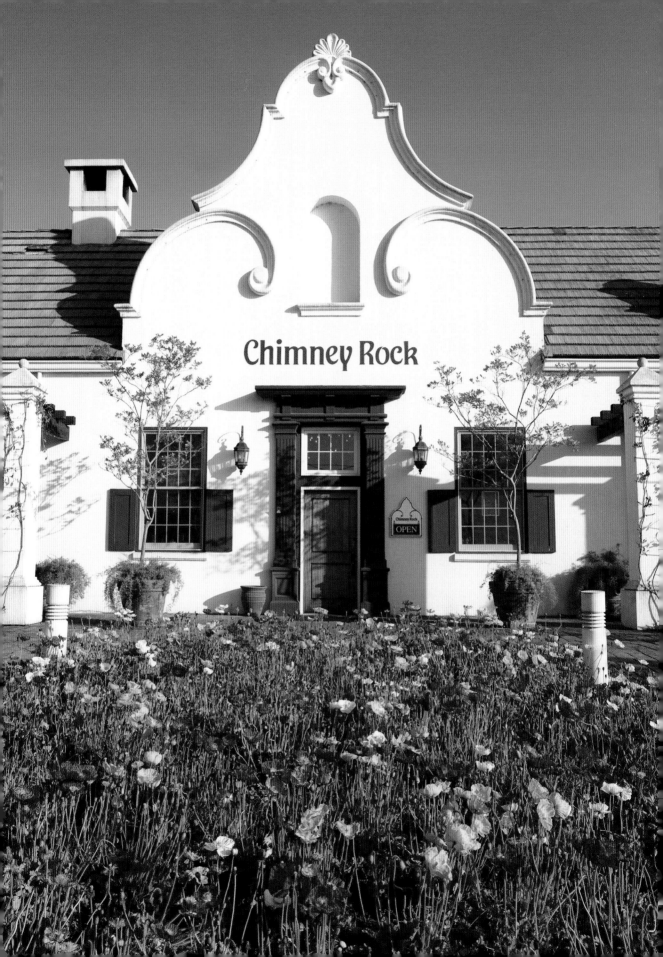

DAVIS ESTATES

On a late-winter afternoon in 2010, Mike Davis parked his pickup on a brushy Calistoga hillside east of the Silverado Trail. Surrounded by manzanitas, madrones, and other trees half encircling a dilapidated 1916 barn and ten or so acres of unkempt vines, he gazed west and contemplated the surreal play of the shadows on the Mayacamas Mountains. Captivated by the scene and already sensing the declining spread's potential, he called his wife, Sandy, telling her "this is the place." Within a few months, the couple had purchased two contiguous woodsy parcels and set about transforming the combined 155-acre property into a world-class winery.

Six years later, hosts in the Davis Estates reception area began drawing open two heavy steel doors, theatrically revealing the same view Davis found so beguiling, though with a key difference. Visitors now savor it from the second-floor terrace of a stunning indoor-outdoor tasting room whose sliding glass doors open up to a vista of well-tended Cabernet Sauvignon and Cabernet Franc and beyond them to other area wineries.

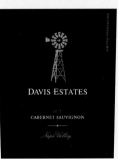

Designed by Howard Backen of Backen Gilliam & Kroeger, one of Northern California wine country's foremost architectural firms, the tasting room simultaneously exudes plush sophistication and down-home comfort. In fine weather, guests sit on the open-air patio on grand swinging wicker sofas suspended from broad cedar beams. A fireplace and a pizza oven anchor opposite ends of the main indoor section. The redwood board-and-batten exterior mimics that of the now restored barn and a new building housing the production facility and offices.

When it came to winemaking, the Davises charted the same nothing-but-the-best course. Cary Gott, a winery specialist who helped establish Round Pond in Rutherford and Ram's Gate in Sonoma, developed the Davis Estates lineup of wines, among them Sauvignon Blanc, Pinot Noir, Cabernet Sauvignon, Cabernet Franc, and the Zephyr Meritage blend of Bordeaux varietals. Philippe Melka, one of the world's premier wine consultants, oversees two subscription-only wines, a Petite Sirah and a Cabernet Sauvignon bearing the label Phase V.

All tastings at Davis Estates are hosted and by appointment only. The sixty-minute Terrace Tasting takes place indoors or outdoors depending on guests' preferences. The Heritage Tour & Tasting, which lasts about ninety minutes, includes a visit to the barn and other sites, as well as a close-up look at the grounds. Guests partaking of the two-hour VIP Experience sip Phase V and top Davis wines in a private room off the main terrace, slipping away briefly for a tour of the 11,000 square feet of caves and portions of the ultra-high-tech production facility.

DAVIS ESTATES
4060 Silverado Trail North
Calistoga, CA 94515
707-942-0700
concierge@davisestates.com
davisestates.com

OWNERS: Mike and Sandy Davis.

LOCATION: 5 miles southeast of downtown Calistoga.

APPELLATIONS: St. Helena, Howell Mountain, Los Carneros, Oakville, Rutherford.

HOURS: 11 A.M.–4 P.M. Tuesday–Sunday, by appointment.

TASTINGS: $60–$225.

TOURS: Some tastings include tours of property or winery, or both.

THE WINES: Cabernet Franc, Cabernet Sauvignon, Chardonnay, Merlot, Petit Verdot, Petite Sirah, Pinot Noir, Sauvignon Blanc, Viognier.

SPECIALTIES: Davis Estates Howell Mountain Cabernet Sauvignon and Zephyr Meritage blend, Phase V Cabernet Sauvignon and Petite Sirah.

WINEMAKERS: Cary Gott, Davis Estates; Philippe Melka, Phase V.

ANNUAL PRODUCTION: 6,000 cases.

OF SPECIAL NOTE: Kugel ball of red South African granite, weighing 2.5 tons, rotates on water in front of hospitality center; water pressure lifts the ball, an artistic representation of a grape, above a base of green granite carved in the shape of a Cabernet leaf. Howell Mountain Cabernet and Zephyr Meritage blend available only in tasting room.

NEARBY ATTRACTION: Culinary Institute of America at Greystone (cooking demonstrations).

33

DOMAINE CARNEROS

DOMAINE CARNEROS
1240 Duhig Rd.
Napa, CA 94559
800-716-BRUT (2788)
707-257-0101
domainecarneros.com

OWNERS: Partnership
between Taittinger and
Kopf families.

LOCATION: Intersection of
Hwys. 121/12 and Duhig
Rd., 4 miles southwest
of the town of Napa and
6 miles southeast of
Sonoma.

APPELLATION: Los Carneros.

HOURS:
10 A.M.–5:30 P.M. daily.

TASTINGS: $30–$40 for
seated tastings (varies
by tasting selected);
reservations required.

TOURS: 11 A.M., 1 P.M.,
and 3 P.M. daily ($50).

THE WINES: Brut Rosé,
Le Rêve, Pinot Noir,
Vintage Brut.

SPECIALTIES: *Méthode traditionnelle* sparkling wine,
Pinot Noir.

WINEMAKERS: Eileen Crane,
founding winemaker;
TJ Evans, Pinot Noir
winemaker.

ANNUAL PRODUCTION:
48,000 cases.

OF SPECIAL NOTE:
Panoramic views of the
Carneros region. Cheese,
caviar, smoked salmon, and
charcuterie available for
purchase.

NEARBY ATTRACTION:
di Rosa (indoor and
outdoor exhibits of works
by contemporary Bay Area
artists).

An architectural tribute to its French heritage, the impressive Domaine Carneros château would look at home in Champagne, France. Crowning a hillside in the Carneros region of southern Napa, it is situated in a prime growing area for Chardonnay and Pinot Noir, the primary grape varieties used in sparkling wine. A grand staircase framed by fountains and gardens forms the entrance to the winery. French marble floors, high ceilings, and decorative features such as a Louis XV fireplace mantel impart a palatial ambience. Guests savor wines and food pairings seated at their choice of a private table in the elegant salon, warmed by a fireplace on cool days, or on the broad, sunny terrace with its panoramic views of the surrounding vineyards.

Domaine Carneros started with a quest by Claude Taittinger of Champagne Taittinger in Reims, France, for an ideal site in California for growing and producing world-class sparkling wine. He found it in the Carneros, where a long, moderately cool growing season and breezes from San Pablo Bay allow for slow, even ripening, mature flavors, and bright acidity in Pinot Noir and Chardonnay grapes.

Established in 1987, Domaine Carneros now includes five certified organic estate vineyards for a total of 350 acres.

Harvest at Domaine Carneros typically begins in mid-August, when the delicate balance between sugar and acidity is at the optimal point for sparkling wines. Crews head out to pick grapes before dawn, and the fruit is immediately brought to the winery for gentle pressing. Each lot is maintained separately until the perfect blend is determined. At Domaine Carneros, sparkling wines are made in accordance with the rigorous and complex *méthode traditionnelle*, in which secondary fermentation takes place in the bottle. A growing portfolio of fine Pinot Noir still wines has aficionados of the Burgundian varietal praising the winery's production and the expertise of Pinot Noir winemaker TJ Evans.

Heading this multifaceted operation is founding winemaker/CEO Eileen Crane, who has been with Domaine Carneros from the beginning—helping to locate the winery site and develop the vineyards and facilities. In addition to serving as one of California's pioneering women in wine, Crane has led the way in sustainable grape growing and winemaking. Domaine Carneros became the first sparkling winery in the United States to receive organic certification for 100 percent of its estate vineyards.

DUTCH HENRY WINERY

In the mid-1800s, prospector Dutch Henry arrived in the Napa Valley hoping to strike it rich by finding treasure troves of silver and mercury. He turned out to be a terrible prospector, so he switched careers and began to farm the fertile creekside slopes in a canyon that now bears his name. Henry sold produce to travelers and local residents, and as rumor goes, he supplemented his farm income as a highwayman, robbing stagecoaches that traveled along the Silverado Trail.

More than a century later, in 1986, the Chafen family purchased their first vineyard in the Napa Valley and soon thereafter established Chafen Family Vineyards. Since then, the family has farmed various vineyards in the area. In 1991 they purchased property in Calistoga, where they built a new winemaking facility and called it Dutch Henry, after the legendary prospector-turned-highwayman who once roamed the site.

In 1992 Dutch Henry Winery opened its doors with Less and Maggie's son, Scott, as winemaker. Scott Chafen has been at the helm of every vintage since. He was initiated into the wine business at an early age, beginning as a teen tractor driver in one of the family vineyards. After earning a bachelor's degree in philosophy from Occidental College in 1990, Scott worked in France for a year. He then returned to Calistoga, where he worked in the vineyards and also in the cellar of a neighboring winery. At Dutch Henry, he focuses on Cabernet, Syrah, and a red Bordeaux wine, sourcing grapes from the family's various estate vineyards (including nearly two acres of Syrah next to the winery), and also crafts wines using fruit from Napa and Sonoma growers. His popular Three Redheads blend pays homage to his three children—all redheads—who, like their dad in his early years, love to visit the vineyard and can often be seen playing with the resident Airedales, chickens, and other farm animals.

From the beginning, the Chafen family has implemented sustainable practices in the vineyard and winemaking facility. The vineyards, vegetable gardens, and orchards are CCOF (California Certified Organically Farmed), and the winery has produced extra-virgin olive oil for more than two decades. The Chafens installed solar panels and built a 4,500-square-foot aging cave, completed in 2008, to ensure consistent temperature and humidity and to save energy and reduce their carbon footprint.

A visit to Dutch Henry Winery is a peaceful, family-friendly experience. The tasting room shares space with the tank room. Outdoors, guests are invited to picnic at tables near the gardens, play bocce, and stroll around the pleasant grounds, shaded by a grove of ancient oaks that certainly witnessed Dutch Henry's escapades more than a century ago.

DUTCH HENRY WINERY
4310 Silverado Trail
Calistoga, CA 94558
707-942-5771
info@dutchhenry.com
dutchhenry.com

OWNER: Scott Chafen.

LOCATION: 4 miles southeast of Calistoga.

APPELLATIONS: Calistoga, Rutherford, St. Helena, Mendocino, Russian River Valley, Mt. Veeder, Howell Mountain.

HOURS: 10 A.M.–4:30 P.M. daily.

TASTINGS: $25 for 5 wines. Reserve tasting, $85 for wines paired with food, by appointment.

TOURS: Guided cave and winery tours daily by appointment; $45 for tour, tasting, and barrel sample.

THE WINES: Cabernet Sauvignon, Chardonnay, Grenache, Merlot, Petite Sirah, Pinot Noir, Syrah, Zinfandel.

SPECIALTIES: Cabernet Sauvignon, Syrah, Bordeaux blend.

WINEMAKER: Scott Chafen.

ANNUAL PRODUCTION: About 2,000 cases.

OF SPECIAL NOTE: Winery is pet-friendly. Picnic area shaded by mature oak trees; bocce court. Small gift selection. Cave includes small room for reserve tastings and private dining. Estate-grown organic extra-virgin olive oil sold in tasting room. All wines available only in tasting room.

NEARBY ATTRACTIONS: Culinary Institute of America at Greystone (cooking demonstrations); Bothe-Napa State Park; Old Faithful Geyser; Petrified Forest.

EHLERS ESTATE

EHLERS ESTATE
3222 Ehlers Ln.
St. Helena, CA 94574
707-963-5972
info@ehlersestate.com
ehlersestate.com

FOUNDER:
Leducq Foundation.

LOCATION: 3 miles north
of St. Helena.

APPELLATION: St. Helena.

HOURS:
9:30 A.M.–3:30 P.M. daily.

TASTINGS: $35 for 4 wines,
by appointment.

TOURS: Start Your Day
tour and tasting ($35),
9:30 A.M. daily, by
appointment.

THE WINES: Cabernet
Franc, Cabernet Sauvi-
gnon, Merlot, Petit Verdot,
Rosé of Cabernet Franc,
Sauvignon Blanc.

SPECIALTIES: 1886 Cabernet
Sauvignon, J. Leducq
Cabernet Sauvignon.

WINEMAKER:
Kevin Morrisey.

ANNUAL PRODUCTION:
8,000 cases.

OF SPECIAL NOTE: All wines
crafted from estate-grown
grapes. Certified organic
and biodynamic vineyards.
Tasting room in restored
1886 stone barn. Picnic
area amid century-old
olive trees. Bocce ball
court.

NEARBY ATTRACTIONS: Culinary Institute of America
at Greystone (cooking
demonstrations); Bale
Grist Mill State Historic
Park (water-powered mill
circa 1846); Robert
Louis Stevenson Museum
(author memorabilia).

A stone barn built in 1886 stands tall and sturdy amid the vineyards of Ehlers Estate, named for Bernard Ehlers, the Sacramento grocer who commissioned the structure and planted the olive grove whose trees now shade the winery's sandy picnic area and bocce ball court. The rocky, loamy soils found here at the Napa Valley's narrowest section — what locals call "the pinch" between Spring and Glass mountains — are similar to those found in Rutherford but with a key difference. The microclimate of slightly shorter sun exposure caused by the mountains, along with early-evening winds funneling cold air through the pinch, pro-

duces smooth, lush, and, to aficionados, singular Cabernet Sauvignons. The same holds true for all the Ehlers Estate wines.

Following Ehlers's death in 1901, his wife, Anna, ran the winery for a while, then sold it during Prohibition. Over the years, the property was divided up, and it wasn't until a century after Ehlers's arrival that the potential for success with Bordeaux varietals such as Cabernet Sauvignon was real-ized. In 1987 the French entrepreneur and philanthropist Jean Leducq, who parlayed his grandfather's Parisian laundry business into what by the late twentieth century reigned as France's largest family-owned company, purchased seven acres once owned by Ehlers. With his wife, Sylviane, he set about reassembling the original Ehlers estate. By 2001, the couple had restored the Ehlers name to the now forty-two-acre property, and their winery had begun gaining recognition for its small-production wines.

The current winemaker, Kevin Morrisey, developed a reputation for making complex, well-balanced wines at Napa Valley's Stags' Leap Winery and Etude in Carneros. Morrisey handcrafts each Ehlers wine from 100 percent organically and biodynamically farmed grapes grown on the estate. Morrisey believes that this style of farming makes possible the degree of agricultural control and deep connection to the land that producing first-rate wines requires.

Seated, private tastings take place in the remodeled, high-ceilinged barn, which may well be the oldest Napa Valley structure in continuous wine-related use. Light streaming in through well-placed windows and wide french doors creates a brighter than expected atmosphere, and the contemporary paintings and plush sofas and chairs play well off nineteenth-century artifacts (among them a wooden wine press) and off the textures of the original stone walls and rough-hewn redwood. The riveted, zinc-topped tasting bar, installed in 2014, tips the balance in favor of modernity, fittingly so given the green direction that the Ehlers winemaking has taken in recent years.

FRANCISCAN ESTATE

Water cascades in bubbly waves over the twin tiers of the lotus-shaped stone fountain that anchors the front courtyard of high-profile Franciscan Estate. The fountain is one of several architectural grace notes on this lushly landscaped property that recall California's Spanish mission era.

The winemaking practices at Franciscan were instituted in the mid-1970s by an early proprietor, Justin Meyer, also a cofounder of prestigious Silver Oak Cellars. Around this time, Franciscan purchased prime Oakville acreage whose esteemed neighbors these days include Opus One, Silver Oak, and Harlan Estate. Meyer was a pioneer in farming each vineyard block, or section, according to its soil and microclimate, during fermentation and aging, based on the diverse characteristics abandon such artisanal techniques Franciscan still considers it vital

segregating grapes by block and blending the resulting wines that emerged. Wineries often as case production increases, but to making high-quality wines. years, but one of his successors, of exclusive Quintessa, introduced Bordeaux-style red blend. During began making a Chardonnay,

Meyer departed after several Agustin Huneeus, now the owner Magnificat, Franciscan's signature Huneeus's tenure, Franciscan also Cuvée Sauvage, using native yeasts from the vineyard instead of commercial ones. Winemaker since 2003, Janet Myers believes this traditional Burgundian method, rare in California at the time, yields more complex flavors.

Franciscan produces wines from many varietals but at its core it remains a Cabernet Sauvignon house, with the Cabernet-predominant Magnificat and five different Cabernets. The Franciscan-owned Mount Veeder Winery in the western Napa Valley hills also makes several Cabernets, providing tasters the opportunity to compare wines using grapes grown on the warmer, loamier valley floor to ones from cooler-climate mountain fruit from rocky soils. At tastings, all-white and all-red flights are possible, and there's a Mount Veeder–only option. Knowledgeable staffers at the main tasting bar, a convivial, high-ceilinged space with light pouring in through a full-length clerestory window, tailor the descriptions of the wines and Franciscan's history to guests' level of interest. On summer weekends, the mood is even more casual at the adjoining outdoor terrace, furnished with tables and chairs, where wines from the tasting bar are also poured. Visitors seeking to delve deeper can reserve a seated private tasting or participate in a blending or other seminar in one of several clubby, dark-paneled rooms furnished with plush leather chairs.

FRANCISCAN ESTATE
1178 Galleron Rd.
St. Helena, CA 94574
707-967-3830
info@franciscan.com
franciscan.com

OWNER:
Constellation Brands.

LOCATION: 3 miles south of downtown St. Helena.

APPELLATIONS: Oakville, Mt. Veeder, Los Carneros.

HOURS: 10 A.M.–5 P.M. daily.

TASTINGS: $15–$25 for 4–6 wines; $15–$25 for 4–6 current-release, small-production, or reserve wines.

TOURS: Vineyard and barrel tours (including tastings), by appointment.

THE WINES: Cabernet Sauvignon, Chardonnay, Merlot, Port, Rosé of Syrah, Sauvignon Blanc.

SPECIALTIES: Equilibrium and Fountain Court white blends, Franciscan Oakville Estate Cabernet Sauvignon, Magnificat red blend, Mount Veeder Cabernet Franc and Cabernet Sauvignon.

WINEMAKER: Janet Myers.

ANNUAL PRODUCTION: 160,000 cases.

OF SPECIAL NOTE: Rose garden area for picnics. Tastings include wines from Mount Veeder Winery. Franciscan Estate Reserve Lunch with wine pairing (Fridays). Blending and sensory seminars by reservation. Events include Magnificat release party (April), Mount Veeder release party (July), Harvest Party Grape Stomp (October). Twelve small-production wines available only in tasting room.

NEARBY ATTRACTION: Culinary Institute of America at Greystone (cooking demonstrations).

FRANK FAMILY VINEYARDS

FRANK FAMILY VINEYARDS
1091 Larkmead Ln.
Calistoga, CA 94515
800-574-9463
info@frankfamily
vineyards.com
frankfamilyvineyards.com

OWNERS:
Rich and Leslie Frank.

LOCATION: About 5 miles
north of downtown
St. Helena via Hwy. 29.

APPELLATION: Napa Valley.

HOURS: 10 A.M.–5 P.M. daily.

TASTINGS: $30 for sparkling
wine and reserve wines.
Reservations suggested.

TOURS: None.

THE WINES: Cabernet
Sauvignon, Chardonnay,
late-harvest Chardonnay,
Petite Sirah, Pinot Noir,
Port, Sangiovese, sparkling
wine, Zinfandel.

SPECIALTIES: Cabernet
Sauvignon from Ruther-
ford, sparkling wine, Chardonnay from Carneros.

WINEMAKER: Todd Graff.

ANNUAL PRODUCTION:
100,000 cases.

OF SPECIAL NOTE: Picnic
tables for use by visitors.
Reserve Lewis Chardonnay
and Pinot Noir, Sangio-
vese, and Zinfandel;
Rutherford Reserve
Cabernet; Winston Hill
Red Wine; and *méthode
champenoise* wines avail-
able only at winery.

NEARBY ATTRACTIONS:
Bothe-Napa State Park
(hiking, picnicking, horse-
back riding, swimming);
Robert Louis Stevenson
State Park; Old Faithful
Geyser of California; Petri-
fied Forest; Sharpsteen
Museum (exhibits on
Robert Louis Stevenson
and Walt Disney animator
Ben Sharpsteen).

At a time when many Napa Valley wineries are increasingly exclusive, the convivial, unpre-tentious ambience at Frank Family Vineyards is decidedly refreshing. Yet this is not the only reason for heading slightly off the beaten path to reach this historic property. It is home to a massive stone building constructed in 1884, recorded as the third-oldest winery in Napa. Refurbished in 1906 with sandstone from the nearby hills, the structure is listed on the National Register of Historic Places and as an official Point of Historical Interest in the state of California.

In 1990 Rich Frank purchased a home and property in Rutherford as an easy getaway destination from the hustle and bustle of Hollywood during his tenure as president of Disney Studios. With a great hillside vineyard, Winston Hill, already in his portfolio, in 1992 he pur-chased the historic stone winery. He then slowly started to build production by acquiring several additional vineyards in the Napa Valley, including the Benjamin Vineyard in Rutherford, the Lewis Vineyard in the Carneros, and the S&J Vineyard in Napa's Capell Valley. Today the winery owns nearly four hundred acres of vineyards, which winemaker Todd Graff utilizes to produce Frank's wines. While the winery has been credited with leading

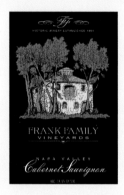

the grower-producer sparkling wine movement in California, the focus at Frank Family Vineyards is largely on still wines. Driving Frank Family's acclaim are four distinct Cabernets and Cabernet blends: the Napa Valley Cabernet, the Rutherford Reserve Cabernet, Winston Hill, and Patriarch. The winery also produces very small quantities of vineyard-designate wines. Carneros Chardonnay is Frank Family's most popular bottling in the United States.

Rich, along with his wife, Leslie, an Emmy Award–winning TV journalist, knows how to make visitors feel welcome. The tasting room, at times brimming with laughter, has been recognized consistently among the best in Napa in Bay Area polls. It has also received critical recognition as *Connoisseurs' Guide to California Wine* "Winery of the Year" and top rankings in the *Wine & Spirits* annual restaurant poll.

Visitors to the tasting room have the option to taste both still and sparkling wines in one of six tasting areas in the yellow Craftsman house. They may also enjoy the grounds, including the picnic tables under the towering elm trees on the property, or the rocking chairs on the front porch. The luckiest guests may even receive a warm welcome from one of the winery's dogs—Riley, a German shepherd, or Bristol, a chocolate lab.

GRGICH HILLS ESTATE

F ew people driving along Highway 29 recognize both of the red, white, and blue flags flying in front of this winery. They certainly know one, the American flag. The other represents Croatia, the native country of winemaker and co-owner Miljenko "Mike" Grgich.

The simple red-tile-roofed, white stucco building may not be as flashy as those of nearby wineries, but as the saying goes, it's what's inside that counts. Once visitors pass beneath the grapevine trellis and into the dimly lit recesses of the tasting room, they forget about exterior appearances. The comfortable, old-world atmosphere at Grgich Hills Estate is not a gimmick.

The winery was founded by Mike Grgich (pronounced "GUR-gitch") and Austin E. Hills on July 4, 1977. Both were already of the Hills Brothers coffee legendary, especially in France. attention in 1976, when, at the all-French panel of judges telena Chardonnay over the in a blind tasting. It was a California wine industry in

well known. Hills is a member family. Grgich was virtually He had drawn worldwide now-famous Paris tasting, an chose his 1973 Chateau Mon- best of the white Burgundies momentous occasion for the general and in particular for

Mike Grgich, who was already acknowledged as one of the state's top winemakers.

Finally in a position to capitalize on his fame, Grgich quickly found a simpatico partner in Hills, who had a background in business and finance and was the owner of established vineyards. The two men shortly began turning out the intensely flavored Chardonnays that remain the flagship wines of Grgich Hills Estate.

Grgich, easily recognizable with his trademark blue beret, was born in 1923 into a winemaking family on the Dalmatian coast of Croatia. He arrived in California in 1958 and spent his early years at Beaulieu Vineyard, where he worked with the late, pioneering winemaker André Tchelistcheff before moving on to Mondavi and Chateau Montelena. Grgich continues to make wine and relies on a younger generation — daughter Violet Grgich, vice president of sales and marketing, and nephew Ivo Jeramaz, vice president of production and vineyard development — to carry on the family tradition. Visitors may well run into family members when taking the exceptionally informative winery tour or while sampling wines in the cool, cellarlike tasting room or in the VIP tasting room and hospitality center.

GRGICH HILLS ESTATE
1829 St. Helena Hwy.
Rutherford, CA 94573
800-532-3057
info@grgich.com
grgich.com

OWNERS: Miljenko "Mike" Grgich and Austin Hills.

LOCATION: About 3 miles south of St. Helena.

APPELLATION: Napa Valley.

HOURS: 9:30 A.M.–4:30 P.M. daily.

TASTINGS: $25 for 5 wines.

TOURS: By appointment, 11 A.M. and 2 P.M. daily.

THE WINES: Cabernet Sauvignon, Chardonnay, Fumé Blanc, Merlot, Violetta (late-harvest dessert wine), Zinfandel.

SPECIALTY: Chardonnay.

WINEMAKER: Mike Grgich.

ANNUAL PRODUCTION: 65,000 cases.

OF SPECIAL NOTE: Behind the scenes tour and tasting by appointment. Grape stomping offered daily during harvest. Napa Valley Wine Train stops at Grgich Hills for special tour and tasting; call 800-427-4124 for schedule. Winery marks 40th anniversary in 2017.

NEARBY ATTRACTIONS: Bothe-Napa State Park (hiking, picnicking, horse-back riding, swimming); Bale Grist Mill State Historic Park (water-powered mill circa 1846); Robert Louis Stevenson Museum (author memorabilia).

HEITZ WINE CELLARS

HEITZ WINE CELLARS
TASTING AND SALES ROOM:
436 St. Helena Hwy. South
St. Helena, CA 94574
707-963-3542

MAILING ADDRESS:
500 Taplin Rd.
St. Helena, CA 94574
heitzcellar.com

OWNERS: Heitz family.

LOCATION: 2 miles south
of St. Helena.

APPELLATION: Napa Valley.

HOURS: 11 A.M.–4:30 P.M.
daily.

TASTINGS: Complimentary.

TOURS: Of winery by
appointment.

THE WINES: Cabernet
Sauvignon, Chardonnay,
Grignolino, Port, Sauvignon
Blanc, Zinfandel.

SPECIALTY: Vineyard-
designated Cabernet
Sauvignon.

WINEMAKERS: David Heitz
and Brittany Sherwood.

ANNUAL PRODUCTION:
40,000 cases.

OF SPECIAL NOTE: Most
vineyards certified organic.
The only Napa Valley
producer of Grignolino,
a red Italian wine grape
commonly grown in the
Piedmont region.

NEARBY ATTRACTIONS:
Culinary Institute of
America at Greystone
(cooking demonstrations);
Bothe-Napa State Park
(hiking, picnicking,
horseback riding,
swimming); Bale Grist
Mill State Historic Park
(water-powered mill
circa 1846); Robert Louis
Stevenson Museum (author
memorabilia).

In 1961, when Joe and Alice Heitz produced their first bottle of wine, they never dreamed that one day Heitz wines would grace dining tables across the country and even around the world. The couple started Heitz Wine Cellars on an eight-acre vineyard just south of St. Helena when Napa Valley had fewer than twelve wineries. As news spread about the quality of the wines, their business grew. In 1964 the Heitzes acquired 160 acres of pristine farmland in the gently sloping hills near the Silverado Trail. This property, which included an historic stone cellar built in 1898, became the heart of their family business.

Two of their earliest visitors were Tom and Martha May, owners of Martha's Vineyard in Oakville. The Heitzes agreed to purchase their fruit, and when Joe Heitz crafted an especially remarkable Cabernet Sauvignon from the 1966 vintage, the two families decided to put the vineyard's name on the bottle, creating the first Napa Valley Cabernet with vineyard designation. Martha's Vineyard Cabernet Sauvignon is now one of the most widely recognized wines in the world, and the Heitz family's exclusive arrangement to produce wine from the Martha's Vineyard grapes continues today. Heitz

Trailside Vineyard and Napa Valley Cabernets have also earned acclaim.

Joe Heitz was a founder of the "new" winery movement. Believing that Napa Valley wines could compete on the world stage, he took the lead in pursuing quality and commanding prices that reflected greater parity with European wines. The Heitz family was also among the first to export their wines. Offering fresh insights and taking bold steps earned Heitz the admiration of generations of California winemakers, as well as induction in 2012 into the Hall of Fame at the Culinary Institute of America.

Second-generation siblings now lead the business. As president, Kathleen Heitz Myers carries on the family legacy of leadership in the wine industry, having served as chair of the California Wine Institute board of directors and president of Napa Valley Vintners. David Heitz has been head of the winemaking team since the 1990s. Third-generation Harrison Heitz is focused on sales and marketing, and has been instrumental in developing the winery's solar energy plan. In 2002, at the site of the original winery, the family built a new sales and tasting room of native stone. On a back patio, visitors can admire panoramic views within feet of the first Cabernet Sauvignon vines. The Heitz family is pleased to celebrate the milestone of their fifty-sixth anniversary as one of the few family-owned wineries established during the renaissance of Napa Valley winemaking.

THE HESS COLLECTION WINERY

A gently winding road heads up a forested mountainside to this winery on the western rim of the Napa Valley. Although only a fifteen-minute drive from bustling Highway 29, the estate feels a thousand times removed. Arriving visitors are greeted with stunning vineyard views from almost every vantage point.

Swiss entrepreneur Donald Hess has owned vineyards on Mount Veeder since 1978, so when he decided to establish his own winery, he didn't have to look far to find the Christian Brothers Mont La Salle property. He already knew that the east side of the extinct volcano provided a cool climate that allowed a long growing season as well as excellent soil drainage — two viticultural components known for producing Cabernet Sauvignon with excellent structure and superb concentration of aromas and flavors. Vineyards were first planted on this land in the 1860s, long before the ivy-clad, three-story stone winery was built in 1903. The Christian Brothers produced wine here for nearly a half century before leasing the facilities to Hess in 1986. He began planting Cabernet Sauvignon vineyards on terrain so steep they have to be picked by hand. The vines must grow extended roots to cling to the mountainside, and the resultant stress creates fruit of exceptional character.

The Hess Collection farms 310 acres of Mount Veeder vineyards that range in elevation from six hundred to two thousand feet. Viewing itself as a steward of the land, the winery farms these vineyards using the principles of sustainable agriculture. The vineyards and winery have been certified by the Napa Green program of the Napa Valley Vintners.

Hess spent three years renovating the facility before opening it to the public in 1989. The overhaul included transforming 13,000 square feet on the second and third floors to display his extensive collection of international art, which consists of 143 paintings, sculptures, and interactive pieces by modern and contemporary artists, among them such luminaries as Francis Bacon, Frank Stella, Anselm Kiefer, Andy Goldsworthy, and Robert Motherwell. One work evokes a particularly strong response for its social commentary. It is Argentinean Leopold Maler's *Hommage 1974*, an eternally burning typewriter created in protest of the repression of artistic freedom.

The tasting room, which shares the first floor with a century-old barrel-aging cellar, is built from a local iron-rich limestone quarried from the property. The stone had been covered with stucco by the Christian Brothers but was inadvertently exposed during the winery's renovation. This is where visitors linger and share their impressions of both the wine and the art.

THE HESS COLLECTION WINERY
4411 Redwood Rd.
Napa, CA 94558
707-255-8584
hesscollection.com

FOUNDER: Donald Hess.

LOCATION: 7 miles west of Hwy. 29.

APPELLATIONS: Mt. Veeder, Napa Valley.

HOURS: 10 A.M. – 5:30 P.M. daily.

TASTINGS: $25 – $50. Various food-and-wine pairings ($35 – $165) offered daily by reservation.

TOURS: Art collection open daily; museum admission is free. Guided tours of winery and collection by appointment.

THE WINES: Cabernet Sauvignon, Chardonnay, Malbec, Petite Syrah, Sauvignon Blanc, Viognier, Zinfandel.

SPECIALTIES: Mount Veeder Cabernet Sauvignon, Chardonnay, Malbec.

WINEMAKERS: David Guffy (Hess), Randle Johnson (Artezin).

ANNUAL PRODUCTION: Unavailable.

OF SPECIAL NOTE: Extensive collection of contemporary art. Many wines available only in tasting room.

NEARBY ATTRACTIONS: di Rosa (indoor and outdoor exhibits of works by contemporary Bay Area artists); Alston Regional Park (hiking).

INGLENOOK

INGLENOOK
1991 St. Helena Hwy.
Rutherford, CA 94573
707-968-1161
800-782-4266
reservations@inglenook
.com
inglenook.com

OWNERS: Coppola fsamily.

LOCATION: About 3 miles
south of St. Helena.

APPELLATIONS: Rutherford,
Napa Valley.

HOURS: Château: 11 A.M.–
5 P.M. daily. Bistro: 10 A.M.–
5 P.M. daily.

TASTINGS: Sit-down tasting
of 4 estate wines paired
with cheese. Reservations
online or via phone
required.

TOURS: Reservations
required (707-968-1161).

THE WINES: Blancaneaux
(premier white blend),
Cabernet Sauvignon,
Edizione Pennino
Zinfandel, RC Reserve
Syrah, Rubicon (premier
red blend), Sauvignon
Blanc.

SPECIALTY: Rubicon.

WINEMAKER:
Philippe Bascaules.

ANNUAL PRODUCTION:
Unavailable.

OF SPECIAL NOTE: Extensive
shop with estate olive oil,
books, wine accessories,
and gifts. More than
200 acres of organically
certified vineyards. Wines
by the glass, espresso, sodas,
and pairing bites offered at
the Bistro Wine Bar.

NEARBY ATTRACTIONS:
Robert Louis Stevenson
Museum (author
memorabilia); Napa Valley
Museum (winemaking
displays, art exhibits);
Culinary Institute of
America at Greystone
(cooking demonstrations).

Inglenook was founded in 1879 by Finnish sea captain Gustave Niebaum, who made his fortune in the Alaska fur trade. He modeled the massive stone château after the estates he had visited in Bordeaux and imported the best European grapevines to plant nearby. Inside the château is an exhibit celebrating milestones in Inglenook's long, illustrious history, including the production of the 1941 Cabernet Sauvignon, heralded as one of the greatest wines ever made.

Seeking a weekend home in wine country, the Coppolas were shown the historic Niebaum mansion in 1975, the start of their thirty-five-year journey to restore the original estate and its label. By acquired the major parcels renamed it Niebaum-vineyards with the same type by the founder in the 1800s château and its grounds back European-style front court-and stone pergola graced with thirty-foot reflecting pool In the vaulted entrance is

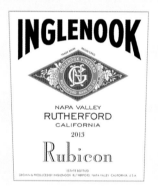

1995, the Coppolas had of the original estate and Coppola. They replanted of rootstock originally used and began bringing the to their former glory. The yard now features a redwood grapevines and a ninety-by-that is illuminated at night. another of Francis Coppola's most dramatic creations: a grand staircase built of exotic hardwoods imported from Belize.

When Coppola set out to craft a proprietary red wine using the acclaimed estate vineyards in 1978, he decided to call it Rubicon, signifying the point of no return. The Bordeaux-style blend remains the winery's premier red wine. In 2011 Coppola acquired the iconic Inglenook trademark, restoring the estate's original name. At the same time, Philippe Bascaules, renowned winemaker from Bordeaux, France, came on board.

Visitors may take part in various tours and tastings, including the Heritage Tasting of current releases and the Rubicon Library Tasting, and numerous private experiences. For something special, the Salon Tasting pairs each wine with bites by the winery chef, served in the intimate Daniel Salon. Inglenook also offers a Bistro Wine Bar with courtyard access and vineyard views, where guests may enjoy wines by the glass paired with tasting bites. The château boasts intimate wine cellars, a barrel room, Infinity Caves, and an extensive retail salon, as well as numerous historical installations that speak to the renowned Inglenook heritage.

JERICHO CANYON VINEYARD

A nineteenth-century toll road rises north a mile from Highway 29 in Calistoga to this serenely secluded winery at the base of Mount St. Helena. Today, as in 1989 when Dale and Marla Bleecher purchased the rocky 135-acre cattle ranch that became Jericho Canyon Vineyard, coyotes, deer, wild turkeys, mountain lions, and the random black bear roam the hillside and forest beyond. The couple saw the potential for winemaking magic at this site that for them recalled Italian hill-country vineyards known for exceptional wines.

Within two years of purchasing the ranch, the Bleechers had planted forty acres of Cabernet Sauvignon, Cabernet Franc, Petit Verdot, and Merlot on the steep terraced slopes that rise east and west from Jericho Creek, which  flows along the canyon floor. Except for the vineyards, the winery, a barn, and a home, the property's surrounding ninety- five acres remain wilderness.

Operating initially as growers, the Bleechers sold grapes to Napa Valley wineries that blended them with other fruit. It wasn't until the late 1990s that a winery, Rudd Estate, released a single-vineyard Jericho Canyon Vineyard blend. The couple already had plans to establish a winery, but the critical acclaim this wine achieved made them all the more determined to make it happen. The redwood-clad winery building, which abuts the vineyard's western rows, was completed in 2006.

Today all the estate's fruit is used to make Jericho wines. David Ramey, an early champion of artisanal winemaking, made the Rudd Jericho Canyon Vineyard wine and the Bleechers' early Jericho Canyon Vineyard wines. That winemakers of the stature of Ramey and more recently Michel Rolland, a Bordeaux specialist with an international clientele, have associated themselves with Jericho Canyon speaks to the superior fruit grown here. Since the 2015 vintage, the lead winemaker has been the couple's son, Nicholas, who works with Rolland to create the blends.

The family's history and their approach to green farming and winemaking are among the topics covered at private tastings available by appointment only. Weather permitting, a brief vineyard walk precedes a tasting, but for a real treat sign up for a tour in the winery's Polaris all-terrain vehicle. With its 30 percent grade, the vineyard's western portion seems almost impossibly sheer, but the eastern side's 55-degree slopes and precisely terraced grapevines hold the real drama. Tastings usually begin with Sauvignon Blanc or Rosé, followed by a Cabernet and Jericho Canyon's proprietary blend, Chimera. Collectively, these wines more than fulfill the promise the Bleechers sensed the Jericho site held for producing wines of character and distinction.

JERICHO CANYON VINEYARD
3322 Old Lawley Toll Rd.
Calistoga, CA 94515
707-331-9076
wine@jerichocanyon
vineyard.com
jerichocanyonvineyard.com

OWNERS: Bleecher family.

LOCATION: 3.25 miles north of downtown Calistoga, off Hwy. 29.

APPELLATIONS: Calistoga, Napa Valley.

HOURS: 10 A.M. – 4:30 P.M. daily, by appointment.

TASTINGS: All visits by appointment only, via email or website.

TOURS: Vineyard and cave tours included with tastings, by appointment only.

THE WINES: Cabernet Sauvignon, Sauvignon Blanc.

SPECIALTY: Estate-grown Cabernet Sauvignon.

WINEMAKERS: Nicholas Bleecher and Michel Rolland.

ANNUAL PRODUCTION: 2,000 cases.

OF SPECIAL NOTE: All wines from estate-grown fruit. Polaris all-terrain vehicle tours by prior arrangement. Olive oil from estate-grown trees available at winery. Multiple local and statewide recognitions for sustainable practices, including Certi-fied Napa Green Winery, Napa Green Land, California Sustainable, Napa County Green Business, and Fish Friendly Farming.

NEARBY ATTRACTIONS: Old Faithful Geyser of California; Robert Louis Stevenson Park (hiking); Sharpsteen Museum (exhibits on writer Robert Louis Stevenson and Walt Disney animator Ben Sharpsteen).

JESSUP CELLARS

JESSUP CELLARS
6740 Washington St.
Yountville, CA 94599
707-944-5620
888-537-7879
info@jessupcellars.com
jessupcellars.com

OWNERS: Dan and
Becky Blue; Roy and
Cheri Eisiminger; Jim
and Kelly Mazzo; Vance
and Jana Thompson;
Judd Wallenbrock.

LOCATION: North end of
downtown Yountville,
near Madison St.

APPELLATION: Napa Valley.

HOURS: 10 A.M.–6 P.M. daily.

TASTINGS: Light Flight, $10
for 3 wines; Classic Flight,
$20 for 6 wines. Guided
Wine and Artisan Cheese
Pairing, $25 for 6 reserve
wines, by appointment.

TOURS: Full-day excursion
to sister wineries, with
lunch, by reservation.

THE WINES: Cabernet Franc,
Cabernet Sauvignon,
Chardonnay, Merlot, Petite
Sirah, Pinot Noir, Sauvi-
gnon Blanc, Zinfandel.

SPECIALTIES: Signature red
blends from Napa Valley
grapes.

WINEMAKER: Rob Lloyd.

ANNUAL PRODUCTION:
8,500 cases.

OF SPECIAL NOTE: Gallery
hosts fine art exhibitions
and cultural events, including Art House Short Film
Series and Art House Ses-
sions (singer-songwriters),
summer music concerts.
All wines available only in
tasting room and online.

NEARBY ATTRACTION: Napa
Valley Museum (art
exhibits, Napa Valley
history).

Contemporary art shows and staffers eager to please attract an upbeat clientele to this gallery and tasting room in downtown Yountville. The bright, high-ceilinged space's convivial vibe—in a recent local poll Jessup's staff was voted Napa and Sonoma's most friendly and knowledgeable—only enhances guests' enjoyment of winemaker Rob Lloyd's small-lot selections. Lloyd, a self-described "California kid" with experience at several top estates, favors fruit-forward "fleshy" wines that are rich and smooth, and exhibit soft tannins.

Best known for Table for Four and Juel, its opulent Bordeaux-inspired red blends, Jessup sells its wines online or in the tasting room rather than in restaurants, fine wine shops, or grocery stores. One benefit of this approach is that although the winery sources grapes from top vineyards throughout the Napa Valley, its wines are well priced.

Table for Four leads with Cabernet Sauvignon, and Juel with Merlot. The traditional Bordeaux blending varietals Cabernet Franc and Petit Verdot might appear in supporting roles, and Lloyd sometimes adds the non-Bordeaux varietal Petite Sirah for structure and spice. Along with the crowd-pleasing Manny's Blend, whose chief component is Zinfandel, Table for Four and Juel anchor Jessup's the Art of the Blend Series of mixed-varietal wines crafted in the old-world tradition of proprietary cuvées, the French term for blends. Soon to be joining the series are two new red blends: Graziella (Cabernet Sauvignon and Sangiovese) and Rougette (predominantly Grenache).

Zinfandel and Pinot Noir are among Jessup's single-varietal wines. The lush Zinfandel, from forty-year-old vines, is the winery's best seller. The Pinot Noir, from Los Carneros AVA, displays the earthy notes one expects from the appellation while retaining the varietal's floral notes. On the lighter side, Jessup produces Sauvignon Blanc and Chardonnay and has recently added Trousseau Gris (aka Gray Riesling) sourced from the last such remaining vineyard in California.

Reservations aren't necessary for standard flights of three or six wines, but call or book online at least a day ahead for a guided tasting accompanied by mixed nuts, artisanal cheeses, and gourmet chocolate. At all the tastings, the staffers are generous with their knowledge of the winery, Lloyd's winemaking philosophy, and the Napa Valley. Seasoned wine lovers and beginners will find this a comfortable place to taste and get tips about where to sip next. The fun at Jessup often continues after the tasting room closes, with gallery openings, a music series, a festival of short films, and other events. For the films, a local chef fires up his wok to pop batches of wildly flavored popcorn.

MARKHAM VINEYARDS

J ean Laurent, a Frenchman from Bordeaux, arrived in California in 1852, drawn by the lure of the 1849 Gold Rush. When his prospecting failed to pan out, he made his way to the city of Napa in 1868 and began growing vegetables. Laurent quickly assessed the high quality of the soil and, being from Bordeaux, realized that Napa Valley was ideally suited to grapevines. Six years later, he opened Laurent Winery in St. Helena, first in a modest wooden structure and later in a meticulously constructed stone cellar, completed in 1879. Only three wineries were operating in Napa Valley at the time—Charles Krug, Schramsberg, and Sutter Home—making Laurent's the fourth oldest in the area.

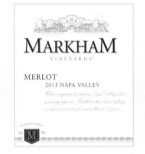

After Laurent died in 1890, number of times, but Laurent's the winery over the years. In 1977 it who had already acquired prime floor, including 93 acres in Yount- The Markham estate vineyards in prime Napa Valley locations. the property changed hands a stone cellar continued to anchor was purchased by Bruce Markham, vineyard land on the Napa Valley ville once owned by Inglenook. now cover a total of 330 acres These vineyards have distinct microclimates that contribute to the complexity of the various wines produced by the winery.

In 1988 the winery and vineyard holdings were sold to Japan's oldest and largest wine company, Mercian Corporation. The winery then went through an ambitious four-year renovation to create more winemaking and storage space, a modern tasting room, and an art gallery. Despite these changes, many things have remained constant. Winemaker Kimberlee Nicholls, who has been with Markham Vineyards for more than twenty years, maintains the winery's focus on producing ultrapremium wines sold at relatively modest prices. Her latest creation, the Cellar 1879 Blend, pays homage to the field blends of Laurent's era by combining the best red varietals from each vintage. It's not uncommon to have up to six different grapes in the blend. Markham Merlot has been the winery's acclaimed powerhouse since its inaugural 1980 vintage. Markham also produces four other nation-ally distributed wines and an extensive portfolio of limited-production and single-vineyard wines.

Stylistically, the visitor center and winery combine both historic and modern elements, with the old stone and concrete facade and the subdued red metal roofing supported by round wooden columns. Koi ponds flank the approach to the tasting room, and beyond them, orange and yellow canna lilies provide bursts of color when the plants bloom in spring and summer. The tasting room has a large fireplace to warm visitors on cold days and an outdoor terrace to enjoy on sunny days. The Markham Gallery features artwork and photography by noted artists.

MARKHAM VINEYARDS
2812 St. Helena Hwy.
North
St. Helena, CA 94574
707-963-5292
markhamvineyards.com

OWNER: Mercian Corporation.

LOCATION: 1 mile north of St. Helena on Hwy. 29.

APPELLATION: Napa Valley.

HOURS: 10 A.M.–5 P.M. daily.

TASTINGS: $20–$30 for current releases and library and estate selections.

TOURS: By appointment.

THE WINES: Cabernet Franc, Cabernet Sauvignon, Cellar 1879 (red blend), Charbono, Chardonnay, Malbec, Merlot, Petit Verdot, Sauvignon Blanc, Syrah, Zinfandel.

SPECIALTY: Merlot.

WINEMAKER: Kimberlee Jackson Nicholls.

ANNUAL PRODUCTION: 100,000 cases.

OF SPECIAL NOTE: Visitor center, home of Markham Gallery, hosts ongoing exhibits. Dinners in historic stone cellar by appointment.

NEARBY ATTRACTIONS: Bothe-Napa State Park (hiking, picnicking, horseback riding, swimming); Bale Grist Mill State Historic Park (water-powered mill circa 1846); Culinary Institute of America at Greystone (cooking demonstrations); Silverado Museum (Robert Louis Stevenson memorabilia).

MATERRA|CUNAT FAMILY VINEYARDS

MATERRA|CUNAT FAMILY VINEYARDS
4326 Big Ranch Rd.
Napa, CA 94558
707-224-4900
info@materrawines.com
materrawines.com

OWNERS: Brian and
John Cunat.

LOCATION: 1.3 miles east of
Hwy. 29 and .9 mile west
of Silverado Trail.

APPELLATIONS: Oak Knoll
District of Napa Valley,
Howell Mountain, Diamond
Mountain District, Calistoga,
St. Helena, Rutherford.

HOURS: 10 A.M.–4 P.M. daily,
by appointment.

TASTINGS: $25 for 5 or 6
wines. $50 for reserve tasting
of 5 or 6 wines (48-hour
advance notice required).

TOURS: 11 A.M.–3 P.M. daily,
by appointment.

THE WINES: Cabernet Sauvignon, Chardonnay, Merlot,
Midnight (red blend of
predominantly Petit Verdot
and Malbec), Petite Sirah,
Sauvignon Blanc, Viognier.

SPECIALTY: Merlot-based
blends.

CONSULTING WINEMAKERS:
Bruce Regalia and Michael
Trujillo.

ANNUAL PRODUCTION:
6,000–7,000 cases.

OF SPECIAL NOTE: Historic
site. Winery is pet-friendly.
Interactive demonstration
vineyards. Occasional
educational tours and
tastings. Japanese-style
bidets in restrooms. Gallery
with rotating exhibits, small
gift shop, library room for
reserve tasting.

NEARBY ATTRACTION: Napa
Valley Museum (winemak-
ing displays, art exhibits).

Brian Cunat grew up on a farm in Illinois, where he developed a strong work ethic and a deep respect for farming and agriculture. While building a successful international real estate business and serving as the youngest president of Kiwanis International, he and his wife, Miki, a native of Japan, traveled the world. Along the way, they toured wineries, ambled through vineyards, and developed a passion for international cuisine paired with world-class wines. In 2007 Cunat decided to combine his love of wine and his farming experience by purchas-

ing a fifty-acre property in the Oak Knoll District of Napa Valley, where Chardonnay vines had flourished for more than a century. He named it Cunat Family Vineyards, gathered an expert team of vineyard managers and winemakers, and planted Merlot, Petit Verdot, Malbec, Chardonnay, Sauvignon Blanc, and Viognier vines with the aim of producing exceptional fruit to transform into first-rate wines.

Cunat also built a cutting-edge winery that opened in 2015. Coined from two Latin words, *mater* (mother) and *terra* (earth), the name reflects the family's commitment to nurturing Mother Earth's gifts of sun, soil, water, and all the elements that contribute to a successful growing season. The vineyards are mostly dry-farmed using environmentally sustainable methods. The facility features state-of-the-art equipment and embraces the very latest technology for production, storage, and hospitality, designed to produce little to no waste and the least possible impact on the planet.

Members of the Cunat family are involved in all facets of the business. Brian and Miki's daughter, Neena, has worked in Napa since 2007 and oversees daily operations. Her younger sister designed the wine labels and interior decoration. Brian's brother, John, and the extended Cunat family are supportive investors. The family participates actively in the winemaking process, guided by well-known consulting winemakers Bruce Regalia and Michael Trujillo, each with more than thirty years in the business. Regalia's experience includes winemaking duties at Duckhorn Wine Company and Goldeneye in Anderson Valley. Trujillo learned alongside legendary winemakers André Tchelistcheff, Tony Soter, and Jim Allen and currently directs the wine program at Sequoia Grove Winery in Napa.

The minimalist interior, with stainless steel embellishments and polished concrete floors, is designed to encourage a focus on the wines. Staffers pour samples at a counter in the main tasting room and at rustic hemlock tables in a private tasting room. Native and drought-tolerant landscaping graces the exterior. On fair-weather days, visitors can relax on the patio at umbrella-shaded tables, surrounded by panoramic views of the Mayacama and Vaca mountains.

MUMM NAPA

For connoisseurs of Champagne, relaxing outdoors on a sunny day with a glass of bubbly, in the company of good friends, taking in a panoramic vineyard view, may be the ultimate pleasure. This is obviously what Champagne Mumm of France had in mind when in 1979 it dispatched the late Guy Devaux to North America to establish a winery that could develop a sparkling wine that would live up to Champagne standards.

Devaux, a native of Epernay, the epicenter of France's Champagne district, was an expert on *méthode champenoise.* In making, the wine under-fermentation in the very poured. After crisscrossing years conducting research, Valley, with its varied soils this French style of wine-goes its bubble-producing bottle from which it will be the United States for four Devaux decreed the Napa and hot summer days and

cool evenings and early mornings, the locale most capable of producing grapes with the acidity required of distinguished sparkling wines.

As founding winemaker, Devaux established the house style of blending wines from numerous sources, and his current successor, Ludovic Dervin, continues the tradition. Mumm Napa prides itself on its relationships with more than fifty noteworthy growers, some of whom have been farming for five generations. Dervin, a Champagne native with experience at wineries in both France and California, blends wines made from individual grape lots to create widely distributed offerings such as Mumm Napa's signature Brut Prestige and rarer ones that include the vintage-dated series DVX—Devaux's name minus the vowels. Mumm Napa also honored Devaux by naming its sole single-vineyard bottling, Devaux Ranch, after him, along with the Carneros site where the wine's Chardonnay, Pinot Noir, and Pinot Meunier grapes are grown.

DVX wines—equal parts Chardonnay and Pinot Noir—are the centerpiece of seated Oak Terrace tastings, shaded by large crimson umbrellas and the outstretched branches of a nearly two-century-old blue oak tree. A plate of cheeses, nuts, and fresh and dried fruit accompanies the wines. Flights and wines by the glass are poured in the light-filled salon and on the adjoining open-air patio. Mumm Napa's tours cover the sparkling winemaking process, including grape varietals and vineyard management, fermentation, blending, bottling, aging, and *dosage*, the process of adding wine mixed with pure sugar to create the requisite residual sugar level for the type of wine (drier or sweeter) being made. Tours conclude at the photography gallery, which displays twenty-seven original Ansel Adams prints and presents exhibitions of other well-regarded photographers' works.

MUMM NAPA
8445 Silverado Trail
Rutherford, CA 94573
707-967-7700
mumm_info@mumm
napa.com
mummnapa.com

OWNER: Pernod Ricard USA.

LOCATION: East of
Rutherford, 1 mile south
of Rutherford Cross Rd.

APPELLATION: Napa Valley.

HOURS: 10 A.M.–6 P.M. daily
(last seating at 5:45 P.M.).

TASTINGS: $20 and up for
flights, $10 and up by the
flute, $50 and up for Oak
Terrace tasting.

TOURS: 10 A.M., 11 A.M.,
1 P.M., and 3 P.M. daily.

THE WINES: Blanc de Blancs,
Brut Prestige, Brut Reserve,
Brut Rosé, Demi-Sec, DVX,
Sparkling Pinot Noir.

SPECIALTIES: Sparkling wine
made in traditional French
style; Devaux Ranch single-
vineyard estate sparkling
wine.

WINEMAKER:
Ludovic Dervin.

ANNUAL PRODUCTION:
250,000 cases.

OF SPECIAL NOTE: Collection
of Ansel Adams photography
and exhibitions of works by
renowned photographers
(free admission). Majority
of wines available only at
winery. Limited availability
of large-format bottles at
winery.

NEARBY ATTRACTION:
Napa Valley Museum
(winemaking displays,
art exhibits).

PEJU

PEJU
8466 St. Helena Hwy.
(Hwy. 29)
Rutherford, CA 94573
707-963-3600
800-446-7358
info@peju.com
peju.com

OWNERS: Anthony and
Herta Peju.

LOCATION: 11 miles north
of the town of Napa.

APPELLATIONS: Rutherford,
Napa Valley.

HOURS: 10 A.M.–6 P.M. daily.

TASTINGS: $35.

TOURS: Self-guided or by
appointment.

THE WINES: Cabernet Franc,
Cabernet Sauvignon,
Chardonnay, Merlot, Petit
Verdot, Provence, Rosé,
Sauvignon Blanc, Syrah,
Zinfandel.

SPECIALTIES: Reserve
Cabernet Sauvignon,
Reserve Cabernet Franc,
Sauvignon Blanc, Fifty/fifty
(red blend).

WINEMAKER: Sara Fowler.

ANNUAL PRODUCTION:
35,000 cases.

OF SPECIAL NOTE: Wine-
and-food pairings, cooking
classes, gift boutique. Barrel
tasting by reservation. Art
gallery featuring work by
contemporary artists. Many
wines available only at
winery.

NEARBY ATTRACTIONS: Robert
Louis Stevenson Museum
(author memorabilia);
Napa Valley Museum
(winemaking displays, art
exhibits); Culinary Institute
of America at Greystone
(cooking demonstrations).

S potting Peju, even on a winery-lined stretch of Highway 29, is easy, thanks to a fifty-foot-tall tasting tower topped with a distinctive copper roof. The tasting tower, like the rest of the property, looks as if it could have been transplanted directly from the countryside of southern France.

The Rutherford estate had been producing wine grapes for more than eighty years when Anthony and Herta Peju bought it in 1983. The couple has been improving the thirty-acre property ever since, honing vineyard techniques and adding Merlot and Cabernet Franc grapes to the estate's core product, Cabernet Sauvignon. By the mid-1990s, demand for Peju wines outstripped the winery's supply. To satisfy it, the Pejus acquired a 350-acre property in northern Napa County in Pope Valley, planted a variety of grapes, and named it Persephone Vineyard, after a goddess in Greek mythology.

Anthony Peju had been living in Europe when he was lured by the movie industry to Los Angeles, where he met Herta Behensky, his future wife. Peju established his own nursery, but had long dreamed of owning a farm. The vibrant towns in Napa Valley and their proximity to San Francisco motivated him to begin a search for vineyard property that ended two years later with the acquisition of what would become Peju Province Winery.

Peju's horticultural experience, combined with his wife's talent for gardening, resulted in two acres of immaculately kept winery gardens. Together, they established a dramatic series of outdoor rooms linked by footpaths and punctuated with fountains and marble sculpture. Hundreds of flowering plants and trees create an aromatic retreat for the Pejus and their visitors. Lining both sides of the driveway are forty-foot-tall sycamore trees, their trunks adorned by gnarled spirals. Visitors reach the tasting room by crossing a small bridge over a pool with fountains. An entrance door of Brazilian cherrywood opens onto a naturally lighted room where three muses grace a century-old stained-glass window.

After more than thirty years, Peju remains a small, family-owned winery with two generations working together. Since 2001, elder daughter Lisa has traveled the world representing Peju wines and reaching out to younger customers. Ariana, who joined the team in 2006, has spearheaded such environmental initiatives as installing enough solar panels to provide 40 percent of the energy for the winery (now a Napa Green Certified Winery), earning organic certification at Peju's Rutherford estate, and practicing sustainable farming at the winery's other two properties.

PINE RIDGE VINEYARDS

Located along a viticulturally charmed stretch of the Silverado Trail, in the shadow of the Stags Leap Palisades, Pine Ridge Vineyards was founded in a farmhouse in 1978. Just two years earlier, the Judgment of Paris wine tasting had deemed a Cabernet Sauvignon from a neighboring Silverado Trail winery to be superior to its French competitors. That triumph spotlighted the Stags Leap District, which was officially recognized as an appellation in 1989.

Pine Ridge owns forty-seven acres within the district, with additional vineyards in the Carneros, Oakville, Rutherford, and Howell Mountain appellations. Winemaker Michael Beaulac crafts Cabernets from all these appellations except Carneros, where the winery's Merlot and Chardonnay are grown.

Having formerly consulted on wines sourced from the vineyards of Languedoc-Roussillon and Châteauneuf-du-Pape in France, Beaulac understands the elemental truth that wine is not merely made, but grown, in the vineyard. The light touch he displays during the winemaking process allows the unique characteristics of each vineyard site to shine through. A highlight of a tasting here is the chance to divine, for instance, the subtle variations between a Stags Leap District Cabernet and an Oakville one, and how Rutherford's celebrated loamy soils yield yet another distinctive set of flavors. In addition to the appellation-specific wines, Beaulac makes Napa Valley–designated Cabernets with grapes from two or more of the Cabernet-producing appellations, along with the flagship Fortis Cabernet Sauvignon, a blend of the best fruit from all four.

A driveway off the Silverado Trail passes between lawns and pocket gardens offering seating with views of the twenty-seven-acre Pine Ridge Estate Vineyard. A rough-hewn pergola shelters plaques describing the six trellising systems displayed in the adjacent demonstration vineyard's semicircular rows. To the pergola's north lies the winery, its simple architecture a reflection of its farmhouse beginnings.

The tasting room's french doors open onto a carpeted salon with muted colors, partial walls of stone, and a tasting bar of dark Honduran mahogany and polished black granite. Through a glass wall fitted with transparent doors, visitors can see into the original barrel room, a softly lit gallery where wine quietly ages. An additional 4,600 French oak barrels rest in the winery's caves, which comprise nearly a mile of underground tunnels. At the end of one chamber, the cool air and subdued lighting interrupted only by a dramatically illuminated art-glass installation by renowned sculptor Dale Chihuly amplify the spirit of a mysterious tropical grotto. Outside the caves, the sun shines on the vineyards, ripening the world-famous Cabernet of the Stags Leap District.

PINE RIDGE VINEYARDS
5901 Silverado Trail
Napa, CA 94558
707-252-9777
800-575-9777
concierge@pineridgewine.com
pineridgevineyards.com

OWNER: Crimson Wine Group.

LOCATION: 4 miles southeast of Yountville.

APPELLATION: Stags Leap District.

HOURS: 10:30 A.M.–4:30 P.M. daily.

TASTINGS: $40 for Estate Tasting of 5 wines. Private tasting of appellation wines in Wine Club Lounge paired with small bites, daily, by appointment, $95. Taste on the Terrace, $60 for 5 wines with appetizers, seasonally, by appointment.

TOURS: Cave walk, barrel tasting, and seated tasting with cheese pairing ($50), daily at 10 a.m., 12 p.m., and 2 p.m. Reservations required.

THE WINES: Cabernet Sauvignon, Chardonnay.

SPECIALTIES: Appellation-specific estate Cabernet Sauvignon, Fortis (multi-appellation Cabernet Sauvignon).

WINEMAKER: Michael Beaulac.

ANNUAL PRODUCTION: 32,000 cases.

OF SPECIAL NOTE: Garden and terrace for tastings. Demonstration vineyard. Many wines available in tasting room only.

NEARBY ATTRACTION: Napa Valley Museum (winemaking displays, art exhibits).

Provenance and Hewitt Vineyards

PROVENANCE AND HEWITT VINEYARDS
1695 St. Helena Hwy.
Rutherford, CA 94573
707-968-3633
866-946-3252
provenance.info@
provenancevineyards.com
provenancevineyards.com

OWNER: Treasury Wine Estates.

LOCATION: 1 mile north of downtown Rutherford.

APPELLATION: Rutherford.

HOURS: 10 A.M.–5 P.M. daily.

TASTINGS: $25 for Provenance Classic Tasting of 4 or 5 wines; $30 for Provenance Reserve Tasting of 5 wines; $75 for Hewitt Reserve Tasting of 3 vintages, by appointment.

TOURS: By appointment.

THE WINES: Cabernet Franc, Cabernet Sauvignon, Malbec, Merlot, Port, Rosé of Malbec, Sauvignon Blanc.

SPECIALTIES: Hewitt Cabernet Sauvignon, single-vineyard Cabernet Sauvignons.

WINEMAKER: Trevor Durling.

ANNUAL PRODUCTION: 55,000 cases (Provenance); 3,900 cases (Hewitt).

OF SPECIAL NOTE: Outdoor lounge. Guests welcome to play Jenga Giant and cornhole. All Hewitt wines and most Provenance wines available only in tasting room.

NEARBY ATTRACTIONS: Culinary Institute of America at Greystone (cooking demonstrations); Bale Grist Mill State Historic Park (water-powered mill circa 1846); Robert Louis Stevenson Museum (author memorabilia).

A sprawling wine-red winery backed by the Mayacamas Mountains catches the eye along its stretch of Highway 29 in the Rutherford appellation's northern section. The sun here shines brilliantly, highlighting tightly spaced, light green rows of Sauvignon Blanc and Semillon grapevines extending westward from the railroad tracks that parallel the highway to the mountains' greener, forested foothills.

The Sauvignon Blanc, its fruit more concentrated because of the vine spacing, is often the first wine poured in the Provenance tasting room. Light streaming through the room's arched windows reflects off the highly polished floor, made from the staves of the oak barrels—complete with their coopers' marks—used to age

the winery's first (1999) vintage. As the building's color suggests, a visit to Provenance is mostly about reds, more than half of which are Cabernet Sauvignons made from grapes sourced from notable Rutherford and Oakville vineyards. Hewitt Vineyard, another label housed at the same winery, offers appointment-only tastings in an intimate room off the main Provenance space. Hewitt releases a single Cabernet Sauvignon each year from estate grapes grown west of the Sauvignon Blanc. The fifty-seven-acre Hewitt vineyard produces distinguished Cabernets year after year, wines that became all the more coveted after *Wine Spectator* magazine ranked the 2010 vintage the number four wine worldwide.

Trevor Durling oversees production of both labels. A graduate of the UC Davis viticulture and enology program, Durling embraces the latest advances in viticultural science and technology. Aerial photography and computer graphics, for instance, allow him and vineyard crews to analyze rows vine by vine to diagnose weak spots and make watering, leaf-pruning, and other adjustments. Come harvesttime, though, Durling's methods turn strictly old-school: he decides when to pick the grapes by how they taste and opts for a rigorous hand-sorting regime to remove stems, overripe grapes, and other unwanted material before fermentation.

Some of the activities of Durling and his wine-cellar crew can be observed through a large semicircular window at the rear of the tasting room. When the workers open the cellar's back doors, the cameo view of the estate vineyards behind them extends back to the Mayacamas. In mid-2014 the winery opened an instantly popular outdoor lounge out front that has views east to the Vaca Range. Shaded by umbrellas and seated on comfortable patio furniture, lounge guests can enjoy one of the Provenance tastings or purchase wines to sip by the glass or the bottle.

Reynolds Family Winery

The winemaking bug bit Oklahoma native Steve Reynolds at an early age, when his dad's business ventures brought the family to a small town in southern Germany for seven years. Reynolds's father was an avid wine collector, and most of the family outings centered around wine and wineries. After high school, Reynolds returned to the United States, earned a degree in dentistry, and set out his shingle in the Lodi-Stockton area in California's Central Valley, where he met his future wife, Suzie.

In 1993 the couple decided that they loved spending time in Napa and wanted to live there. Reynolds sold his practice and  started a new one in Napa, at first thinking he would make wine in his garage as a hobby. The Reynolds family jumped into the wine busi- ness in earnest in 1995, when they purchased an old chicken farm on the Silverado Trail, south of the prestigious Stags Leap District. They planted vineyards and, in 1999, made their first wines from a small portion of a few specific vines. These were shared by friends and family who declared the wines a great success. Buoyed by these accolades, the Reynolds decided to venture into the wine business in a larger, more serious fashion.

The Reynolds Family Winery's first release of around 2,000 cases came at the start of the new millennium, and around that time, Steve Reynolds decided to give up his dental practice so that he could operate the winery full-time. He took courses at UC Davis for two years to perfect his wine-making techniques and credits renowned Napa Valley winemaker Anthony Bell for guiding him through his winery's evolution. Today, Reynolds Family Winery continues to focus on Cabernet, and production has grown to around 7,000 cases. Reserve wines include the winery's Stags Leap District Merlot and Reserve Cabernet Sauvignon, and a limited-production wine, The Quote, which uses an Italian process called *purevino* to minimize sulfite content. Steve Reynolds is also active in two other winery ventures: a whimsical brand called Naughty, and Italics, which produces luxury wines such as the innovative Sixteen blend, which combines grapes sourced from Napa's finest growing districts.

Visitors can sample the latest vintages at the pastoral fourteen-acre estate. Tastes are poured in the intimate tasting room, remodeled in 2016, and at tables flanked by soft leather sofas and easy chairs near the stone fireplace, a popular venue on cool-weather days. Flights are also served outdoors on the spacious veranda, overlooking the estate Cabernet vineyard and a pond that attracts great blue herons, migratory birds, and other wildlife—a bucolic scene redolent of the German wine country landscapes that ignited Steve Reynolds's passion for winemaking as a young boy.

Reynolds Family Winery
3266 Silverado Trail
Napa, CA 94558
707-258-2558
info@reynoldsfamilywinery
.com
reynoldsfamilywinery.com

Owners: Steve and Suzie Reynolds.

Location: 4.5 miles north of downtown Napa.

Appellations: Los Carneros, Stags Leap District, Napa Valley, Russian River Valley.

Hours: 10 A.M.–5 P.M. daily.

Tastings: Seasonal Sampler Flight, $30; Reynolds Remarkable Reds Flight, $35; Family Classic Flight (reds), $45; Tour and Chef's Pairing, $75; Lunch and Learn Wine Education $125. All tastings by appointment and subject to change.

Tours: Daily, by appointment only.

The Wines: Cabernet Sauvignon, Chardonnay, Merlot, Pinot Noir, Sauvignon Blanc.

Specialties: Napa Valley Cabernet and Cabernet-based blends.

Winemaker: Steve Reynolds.

Annual Production: 7,000 cases.

Of Special Note: Expansive veranda overlooking pond, fountain, vineyards, and mountains. Small gift selection. The Quote (red wine blend with minimal sulfite content) available only in tasting room.

Nearby Attraction: Napa Valley Museum (winemaking displays, art exhibits; Skyline Wilderness Park (hiking, biking, horseback, riding, picnicking).

ROBERT MONDAVI WINERY

ROBERT MONDAVI WINERY
7801 Hwy. 29
Oakville, CA 94562
707-968-2001
888-766-6328
info@robertmondavi
winery.com
robertmondaviwinery.com

LOCATION: About 10 miles
north of the town of Napa.

APPELLATIONS: Oakville,
Napa Valley.

HOURS: 10 A.M.–4:45 P.M.
daily.

TASTINGS: $20 for 4 wines in
main tasting room; $45 for
4 wines or by the glass in To
Kalon Reserve tasting room.

TOURS: Signature Tour and
Tasting, including To Kalon
Vineyard, by reservation
($40); other tours available
seasonally. Foreign-language
tours by appointment.

THE WINES: Cabernet
Sauvignon, Chardonnay,
Fumé Blanc, I Block Fumé
Blanc, Merlot, Moscato
D'Oro, Pinot Noir, To Kalon
Cabernet Sauvignon.

SPECIALTIES: Cabernet
Sauvignon Reserve and
Fumé Blanc Reserve.

WINEMAKER:
Geneviève Janssens.

ANNUAL PRODUCTION:
250,000 cases.

OF SPECIAL NOTE: Private
cellar tasting and 4-course
wine-pairing dinner
available with advance
reservations. Large retail
shop with wine books
and Italian imports; open
10 A.M.–6 P.M. daily. Summer
Festival Concert Series
(July); Cabernet Sauvignon
Reserve Release Party
(September).

NEARBY ATTRACTIONS:
Culinary Institute of
America at Greystone
(cooking demonstrations);
Napa Valley Museum
(winemaking displays,
art exhibits).

Wineries come and wineries go in Napa Valley, but in this fast-paced, high-stakes world, few can challenge the lasting achievements of the Robert Mondavi Winery. Since its inception more than fifty years ago, it has remained in the forefront of innovation, from the use of cold fermentation, stainless steel tanks, and small French oak barrels to the collaboration with NASA employing aerial imaging to reveal the health and vigor of grapevines.

Founder Robert Mondavi's cherished goal of producing wines on a par with the best in the world made his name virtually synonymous with California winemaking. That vision is being

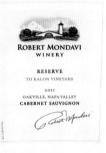

carried out today with ambitious programs such as the To Kalon Project. Named after the historic estate vineyard surrounding the winery, this extensive renovation led to the unveiling of the To Kalon Fermentation Cellar, which capitalizes on the natural flow of gravity to transport wine through the production system. Prized for their ability to enhance aromas, flavors, and complexity in red wines, the cellar's fifty-six French oak fermenting tanks were hand-crafted in Cognac by the renowned cooperage Taransaud. Coopers numbered each stave before disassembling the fermenters for shipping to Oakville, where the team reconstructed them in place at the winery.

Technological advances aside, the best reason for visiting Robert Mondavi Winery is something less tangible: an opportunity to experience the presentation of wine in the broader context of lifestyle. Educational tours and tastings, concerts, art exhibits, and the industry's first culinary programs are all part of the Mondavi legacy. One of the most popular offerings is the Signature Tour and Tasting, which follows the path of the grape from the vine through the cellar to the finished wine. The 550-acre vineyard was named To Kalon (Greek for "the beautiful") by Hamilton Walker Crabb, a winegrowing pioneer who established vineyards here in the late 1800s. It was this property that inspired Robert Mondavi to establish his winery on the site.

The winery's Spanish mission-style architecture, with its expansive archway and bell tower designed by Clifford May, pays homage to the Franciscan fathers who planted the first grapes in the region. Two long wings project from the open-air lobby to embrace a wide expanse of lawn framed by the Mayacamas Mountains on the western horizon. Typical of the winery's commitment to the arts, several sculptures by regional artist Beniamino Benvenuto Bufano (who, like Robert Mondavi's family, came from Italy) are displayed in the courtyard and elsewhere around the grounds. In addition, the winery features art exhibits that change every two months.

ROMBAUER VINEYARDS

The quarter-mile-long drive from the Silverado Trail leads to a winery ensconced in a forest of pine trees. On the far side of the low-slung building, a wide California ranch–style porch affords views that extend to the tree-covered ridge of the Mayacamas Mountains to the west. Without another structure in sight, the serene setting has the ambience of a fairy-tale kingdom secluded from the hustle and bustle of the valley floor. Directly below the winery, a gravel path winds down to a hill where roses are planted in the sun and azaleas thrive in the shade. Scattered about are a half-dozen metal sculptures of fantastical creatures such as a diminutive dinosaur and a life-size winged horse, all weathered to the point that they blend into the landscape.

The Rombauer family traces its heritage to another fertile wine area, the Rheingau region in Germany, where Koerner Rombauer's ancestors made wine. His great-aunt Irma Rombauer wrote the classic book *The Joy of Cooking*. The tradition of linking wine to food is carried on today, with members of the family involved in the operations of the winery, from selecting grapes to marketing the final product.

Koerner Rombauer, a former commercial airline captain, and his late wife, Joan, met and married in Southern California, where both had grown up in an agricultural environment. Since they had always wanted their children to have rural childhood experiences similar to their own, they came to the Napa Valley in search of land. In 1972 they bought fifty acres and settled into a home just up the hill from where the winery sits today. Within a few years, they became partners in a nearby winery. Their hands-on involvement in the winery's operations whetted their appetite for a label of their own and for making handcrafted wines with the passion and commitment of the family tradition. Taking advantage of the topography, the Rombauers built their family winery into the side of the hill. Rombauer Vineyards was completed in 1982.

By the early 1990s, the Rombauers realized they had the perfect location for excavating wine storage caves. Completed in 1997, the double-horseshoe-shaped cellar extends for more than a mile into the hillside. When visitors enter the tasting room, they find a personalized space with an eclectic assortment of memorabilia from Koerner Rombauer's life. Guests may also get an occasional glimpse of another of Koerner's passions—one of the automobiles from his private collection of vintage cars.

ROMBAUER VINEYARDS
3522 Silverado Trail North
St. Helena, CA 94574
800-622-2206
707-963-5170
rombauer.com

OWNERS:
Rombauer family.

LOCATION: 1.5 miles north
of Deer Park Rd.

APPELLATION: Napa Valley.

HOURS: 10 A.M.–5 P.M. daily.

TASTINGS: $25, by
appointment.

TOURS: Cave tours by
appointment.

THE WINES: Cabernet
Sauvignon, Chardonnay,
Merlot, Sauvignon Blanc,
Zinfandel.

SPECIALTIES: Limited-
production and single–
vineyard Cabernet
Sauvignon, Zinfandel,
and Chardonnay; Best
of the Cellar Bordeaux
blend; dessert wines.

WINEMAKER: Richie Allen.

ANNUAL PRODUCTION:
130,000 cases.

OF SPECIAL NOTE: Copies
of the latest edition of
The Joy of Cooking and
other cookbooks by Irma
Rombauer are available
in the tasting room.
Zinfandel Port and Joy, a
late-harvest Chardonnay,
available only at winery.

NEARBY ATTRACTIONS:
Culinary Institute of
America at Greystone
(cooking demonstrations);
Bothe-Napa State Park
(hiking, picnicking,
horseback riding,
swimming); Robert
Louis Stevenson Museum
(author memorabilia).

RUTHERFORD HILL WINERY

RUTHERFORD HILL WINERY
200 Rutherford Hill Rd.
Rutherford, CA 94573
1-800-MERLOT1
707-963-1871
info@rutherfordhill.com
rutherfordhill.com

OWNERS: Terlato family.

LOCATION: About 2 miles south of St. Helena, just north of Rutherford Cross Rd. east of Silverado Trail.

APPELLATION: Rutherford.

HOURS: 10 A.M.–5 P.M. daily.

TASTINGS: Flights available, $25–$40.

TOURS: Cave tour and barrel tasting. Reservations recommended.

THE WINES: Cabernet Franc, Cabernet Sauvignon, Chardonnay, Malbec, Merlot, Petit Verdot, Port, Rosé, Sauvignon Blanc.

SPECIALTIES: Merlot, Bordeaux blends.

WINEMAKER: Marisa Taylor.

ANNUAL PRODUCTION: 40,000 cases.

OF SPECIAL NOTE: Luxury cabanas, patio tastings, and educational cave tours. (Reservations recommended for all special tastings and tours.) Picnic grounds with views. Winery is pet-friendly. Reserve and limited-release wines available only in tasting room.

NEARBY ATTRACTIONS: Culinary Institute of America at Greystone (cooking demonstrations); Robert Louis Stevenson Museum (author memorabilia).

East of the Silverado Trail, a winding mountain road leads to one of Napa Valley's legendary wineries. Here, visitors will find Rutherford Hill Winery, tucked into a hillside and offering a stunning view of the valley. With its gambrel roof and rough-hewn redwood timbers, the winery resembles an antique barn. The impressive building is large enough to house both the winery and the inviting tasting room with its relaxed atmosphere. A pair of gigantic doors greets visitors as they approach the entrance. The winery is framed by expansive lawns and gardens, and a picnic area set in Napa Valley's oldest olive grove.

Rutherford Hill also possesses one of the largest wine-aging cave systems in North America. Begun in 1982 and completed by 1990, the caves are nearly a mile in length. They maintain a natural temperature of 59 degrees Fahrenheit and a relative humidity of 80 percent, conditions that provide the perfect environment and ecologically sensitive way to protect and age the wines. Entering the caves through large doors flanked by towering cypress, visitors immediately notice the heady perfumes of oak and aging Merlot and Cabernet.

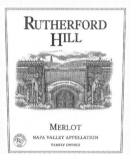

Rutherford Hill Winery was built in 1972 by Joseph Phelps, who soon went on to establish another winery in his own name. In 1976 Bill and Lila Jaeger bought the hilltop property, noting that the region's soils resembled those of Pomerol, a Bordeaux appellation famed for its outstanding Merlot-based wines. The local loam, or "Rutherford dust," a term coined in the late 1930s by famed Russian enologist André Tchelistcheff, is credited with imparting great depth and flavor to the area's plantings of Merlot and Cabernet Sauvignon.

In 1996 Anthony Terlato, a well-known figure in the American fine wine industry, acquired Rutherford Hill with the single-minded goal of producing the finest wines in the Rutherford appellation. Terlato had started his career in his father's Chicago retail wine shop in the 1950s and parlayed a modest business into a leading importer of fine wines. Shortly after purchasing Rutherford Hill, he built a state-of-the-art winery where the winemaker could separately vinify grapes coming from different vineyard lots and grown in many different and idiosyncratic soil types. This allowed the Terlatos and the winemaking team to focus on the specific vineyards producing the finest grapes, including nearly two hundred acres of estate vineyards that are now the foundation of Rutherford Hill wines. Today, Merlot makes up most of the winery's production, underscoring the enduring appeal of wines grown in the renowned Rutherford dust.

SOMERSTON ESTATE

The 1,615-acre Somerston Estate occupies a pristine stretch of Napa Valley's rural paradise, high in the Vaca Mountains ten miles east of the Silverado Trail. The estate was launched in 2004, when winery co-owner Allan Chapman purchased the 660-acre Priest Ranch, named for the first settler of the land, in 1849. In 2005 Chapman added the neighboring Elder Valley, 955 acres that included vineyards planted between 1970 and 1999. Today the estate sustainably farms 215 acres in fourteen vineyard blocks—each bearing the name of a historic clipper ship, for ex-

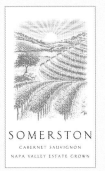

ample, Stornoway, Ariel, Deerhound, Everest, and Gauntlet. (The Chapman family owned and managed Som- erston tea clippers and merchant ships starting in the 1850s.) About four hundred sheep—which play a role in the growing cycle by providing fire and weed abatement—graze in a natural wonderland filled with native oaks and wildlife.

The estate is currently immersed in an ambitious 60-acre replanting program that began in 2010. When it is completed, Somerston will include nearly a hundred distinct, precision-farmed blocks featuring diverse soils, microclimates, and exposures. Somerston sells about 40 percent of its fruit to renowned vintners, but retains the highest-quality grapes (approximately 60 percent) for its own estate vintages. Winemaker Craig Becker focuses mainly on Cabernet Sauvignon production, with fruit grown in 90 percent of the vineyard blocks. He also crafts single-vineyard wines and blends from other Bordeaux varietals, including Cabernet Franc, Merlot, and Sauvignon Blanc. Somerston Estate's most popular bottlings, apart from estate Cabernet Sauvignon wines, include red Bordeaux-style proprietary blends called Stornoway and Deerhound.

The winery facility is located inside a 12,000-square-foot barn equipped with a carbon-neutral cooling, heating, and hot water system. The adjacent tasting room faces an expansive meadow, and a modernist fountain of concrete blocks bubbles on the patio, where staffers pour tastings on fair-weather days. The tasting room interior has a polished concrete floor and echoes a barrel theme with burnished paneling salvaged from an old redwood barn. The oak tasting bar sports hooplike stainless steel straps across the front. Glass panels provide a long view into the attached barrel room.

Guests may also opt to take an extensive tour of the spectacularly beautiful estate in the open-air comfort of an ATV buggy. The route winds past acres of terraced vineyards, which range from 840 to 2,400 feet above sea level, as well as forests, natural springs, and spring-fed lakes. Highlights include several acres of both ornamental and organic vegetable gardens, a recently restored barn that serves as a special event venue, and an island gazebo set in a lake frequented by waterfowl.

SOMERSTON ESTATE
3450 Sage Canyon Rd.
St. Helena, CA 94574
707-967-8414
visit@somerstonestate.com
somerstonestate.com

OWNERS: Allan Chapman, John Wilson, and Craig Becker.

LOCATION: 13 miles east of St. Helena.

APPELLATION: Napa Valley.

HOURS: 11 A.M.–4 P.M. daily, by appointment.

TASTINGS: $75 for 4 wines. Picnic lunch for additional charge available by reservation. One-week advance reservation recommended.

TOURS: ATV buggy tour included with tasting. One-week advance reservation recommended.

THE WINES: Cabernet Franc, Cabernet Sauvignon, Merlot, Sauvignon Blanc.

SPECIALTIES: Limited-production wines made from select vineyard blocks; Stornoway (red Bordeaux-style blend).

WINEMAKER: Craig Becker.

ANNUAL PRODUCTION: 1,500 cases.

OF SPECIAL NOTE: Wine tasting on historic Napa Valley estate. Occasional cooking classes and winemaker dinners at estate. Select wines available only in tasting room.

NEARBY ATTRACTIONS: Lake Hennessey (boating, fishing, camping); Lake Berryessa (boating, fishing, camping, wildlife watching).

STAGS' LEAP WINERY

STAGS' LEAP WINERY
6150 Silverado Trail
Napa, CA 94558
707-257-5790
stagsleap.com

OWNER: Treasury Wine Estates.

LOCATION: 7 miles north of downtown Napa.

APPELLATION: Stags Leap District.

HOURS: By appointment.

TASTINGS: $65 for 5 wines, as part of tour, by appointment.

TOURS: 90-minute Estate Tour and Tasting. Reservations required.

THE WINES: Cabernet Sauvignon, Chardonnay, Merlot, Petite Sirah, Rosé, Viognier.

SPECIALTIES: Cabernet Sauvignon, Ne Cede Malis (old-vine Petite Sirah blend).

WINEMAKER: Christophe Paubert.

ANNUAL PRODUCTION: 100,000 cases.

OF SPECIAL NOTE: One of Napa Valley's oldest wineries. Historic Manor House built in 1892.

NEARBY ATTRACTION: Napa Valley Museum (winemaking displays, art exhibits).

To visit the Manor House at Stags' Leap Winery is to enter a world of Old California–style wealth, set amid 240 acres of pristine countryside. Like an elegant time capsule, the Romanesque mansion evokes the lavish dinners and lawn parties staged by its builder, San Francisco investor Horace B. Chase. Constructed in 1892 of locally quarried stone, the two-story house stands at the end of a driveway lined with fan palms and the low rock walls of terraced gardens. Mortared stone columns support the roof of a wraparound porch, and a castellated half-turret hosts a massive wisteria vine.

The Chases dubbed the estate Stag's Leap, a name attributed to a native Wappo legend of a stag leaping to elude hunters. The mountains behind the property then came to be called the Stags Leap Palisades. Producing wine to sell and share with friends, the Chases introduced the Stag's Leap Winery label in 1893. The Grange family bought the property in 1913 and turned it into a busy resort. The house sat empty from the early 1950s to 1970, when Carl Doumani spent four years restoring it. He revived the Stags' Leap Winery label, and in 1989 the Stags Leap District appellation (sans apostrophe) was recognized.

Visitors are greeted by friendly and informative staff who take them on a tour of the historic Manor House and the grounds. Paths winding among perennial gardens and vegetable beds offer views of the eighty-acre estate vineyard opposite the house. Inside the gracious Manor House, guests enjoy a seated tasting in the formal dining room, where soft light filters through Victorian leaded glass windows. Tastings are also held outdoors on a covered patio.

Bordeaux-born Christophe Paubert joined Stags' Leap Winery as winemaker in 2009, bringing an impressive background including serving as cellar master at the renowned Château d'Yquem in his native France and building a winery and overhauling a large vineyard in Chile. At Stags' Leap, he crafts balanced wines with the district's characteristic depth and soft tannins. His signature is the award-winning The Leap Cabernet Sauvignon made from fruit sourced from a small, distinct vineyard block at the heart of the estate, whose well-drained volcanic soil is one factor that contributes to the reputation of the winery's Cabernet Sauvignon.

Reaching an elevation of 2,000 feet, the Stags Leap Palisades form a small, secluded valley. To find the winery, visitors take an unmarked Silverado Trail turnoff and travel a narrow country road between vineyards and walnut orchards. The effort is worth it—for Stags' Leap Winery glimmers with the magic of that mighty buck.

STERLING VINEYARDS

An eye-catching complex of bright white walls and curved bell towers, Sterling Vineyards crowns a forested volcanic knoll three hundred feet above the Napa Valley floor. The winery, which from a distance could double as a hilltop Greek island monastery, commands sweeping views of the geometric vineyards and foothills below. To reach it, visitors leave their cars in the parking lot and board an aerial gondola—the only one of its kind in the valley—for a solar-powered glide over a glistening pond, pines, and live oaks to a walkway among the treetops.

A self-guided tour encourages visitors to explore the stately facility at their own pace, while strategically stationed hosts  pour wine samples along the way. Illustrated signboards describe points of interest, and motion-activated flat-screen televisions display videos of winemaking activity. Bells from a former tenth-century London church chime on the quarter hour, their rich tones ringing across exterior foot-paths that afford elevated views of the crush pad and fermentation area. Inside the winery, visitors may observe employees at work among stainless steel tanks and peek at some of the winery's 25,000 barrels as they impart delicate flavors to the wine aging within. On the South View Terrace, redwood planters brim with lavender and ornamental grasses, and two sixty-foot-tall Italian cypresses frame the scene to the south. Here, guests sip wine as they take in the panoramic vistas of vineyards, neighboring estates, and parts of the Mayacamas Mountains on the Sonoma-Napa border, where Mount St. Helena rises above the neighboring peaks to an elevation of 4,344 feet.

Englishman Peter Newton, founder of Sterling Paper International, started the winery in 1964, when he bought a fifty-acre pasture just north of the town of Calistoga. He surprised local vintners by planting Merlot—at the time considered a minor blending grape—along with Chardonnay, Cabernet Sauvignon, and Sauvignon Blanc. Five years later, Newton bottled his first wines, which included California's earliest vintage-dated Merlot. In the early 1980s, the winery purchased one thousand vineyard acres on fourteen different Napa Valley ranches, giving the winemaker a broad spectrum of fruit to work with, as well as control over the farming of the grapes. The winery continues to source fruit from these and two hundred additional acres of select Napa Valley vineyards in various appellations such as Calistoga, St. Helena, Rutherford, and Carneros.

Visitors should make touring the hilltop winery their top priority, as it is one of the most memorable experiences in the Napa Valley.

STERLING VINEYARDS
1111 Dunaweal Ln.
Calistoga, CA 94515
800-726-6136, option 1
help@sterlingvineyards.com
sterlingvineyards.com

OWNER: Treasury Wine Estates.

LOCATION: 1 mile southeast of Calistoga.

APPELLATION: Calistoga.

HOURS: 10:30 A.M.–5 P.M. Monday–Friday; 10 A.M.–5 P.M. Saturday–Sunday. Closed Thanksgiving, Christmas, and New Year's Day.

TASTINGS: $30 admission for aerial gondola ride, self-guided tour, 5 wine tastes, and souvenir glass. For additional tastings of reserve and limited-release wines, visit the website.

TOURS: Self-guided.

THE WINES: Cabernet Sauvignon, Chardonnay, Malvasia Bianca, Merlot, Pinot Noir, Sauvignon Blanc.

SPECIALTIES: Malvasia Bianca, Cabernet Sauvignon, Platinum (Bordeaux blend).

WINEMAKER: Harry Hansen.

ANNUAL PRODUCTION: Unavailable.

OF SPECIAL NOTE: Display of Ansel Adams photographs and wine-related art.

NEARBY ATTRACTIONS: Robert Louis Stevenson Museum (author memorabilia); Napa Valley Museum (winemaking displays, art exhibits).

STORYBOOK MOUNTAIN VINEYARDS

STORYBOOK MOUNTAIN VINEYARDS
3835 Hwy. 128
Calistoga, CA 94515
707-942-5310
colleen@storybookwines
.com
storybookwines.com

OWNERS: Jerry and
Sigrid Seps.

LOCATION: 4.5 miles northwest of Calistoga, .25 mile
before the Sonoma County
line.

APPELLATIONS: Calistoga,
Napa Valley.

HOURS: 10 A.M.–4 P.M.
Monday–Saturday, by
appointment.

TASTINGS: $25 for 4 or 5
wines (includes tour).

TOURS: Included with
tasting.

THE WINES: Cabernet
Sauvignon, Viognier,
Zinfandel.

SPECIALTIES: Estate-grown
Cabernet Sauvignon and
Zinfandel. Antaeus blend
of Zinfandel and Cabernet.

WINEMAKERS: Jerry Seps,
Colleen Seps-Williams.

ANNUAL PRODUCTION:
5,000 cases.

OF SPECIAL NOTE: Certified
100 percent organic estate-
grown grapes. Tastings
held in 130-year-old hand-
dug wine-aging caves.
Listed 13 times in *Wines &
Spirits* magazine's top 100
wineries of the world.

NEARBY ATTRACTIONS:
Old Faithful Geyser of
California; Robert Louis
Stevenson Park (hiking).

Redwoods, oaks, pines, and firs provide the backdrop for the sharply sloped vineyards of this family-run winery that's as unassuming as its Mayacamas Mountains setting is grand. Storybook, at the far northern end of Napa Valley, feels of another era, and not merely because Zinfandel, not Cabernet, is the focus. The forty-two acres of organically farmed vines, which produce wines of such high quality they've been poured at five White House state dinners, occupy a bowl oriented north and east, as if deliberately turning its back on the valley and its hoopla.

Time retreats the moment guests arrive and a host directs them to a grove whose tall redwoods still bear scars from the 1964 fire that destroyed a predecessor vineyard. The winery's moniker, bestowed by its current owners, Jerry and Sigrid Seps, playfully salutes the two German brothers named Grimm who made wines here in the nineteenth century.

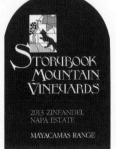

The Grimms hired Chinese laborers to hand-dig two aging caves, which along with a third added later were the sole survivors of the 1964 conflagration. By 1976, when the Sepses purchased the 120-acre estate, it was overrun with postfire vegetation. Jerry, a professor of European history who jokes that he forsook tenure for a tractor, followed precisely the strategy one might expect of an academic endeavoring to determine which grapes to plant: he conducted prodigious research and consulted experts. The latter included the late André Tchelistcheff, one of the Napa Valley's most respected winemakers, who advised him that Zinfandel would thrive best in the property's clay-loam soils.

Tchelistcheff's assessment proved instantly correct. The first two Storybook releases, 1980 and 1981 wines, placed first and second out of two hundred Zinfandels in a San Francisco Bay Area competition. Over time, Jerry identified areas suitable for growing Cabernet Sauvignon and has since planted that grape and other Bordeaux varietals, along with the white grape Viognier, which is bottled separately and blended into one of the Zinfandels. The Bordeaux varietals go into an estate Cabernet and are combined with Zinfandel to make the satisfyingly complex Antaeus red blend. In recent years, Jerry has come to share winemaking duties with his daughter, Colleen Seps-Williams.

That Storybook is the product of deep passion becomes apparent on the short vineyard walk that precedes informal tastings in the low-lit aging caves. Often conducting the tour is Colleen's husband, Rick, who describes Jerry's detailed records of soil types, microclimates, and other characteristics. Armed with this data, Jerry carefully farms the land with the same family he hired more than four decades ago, a sign of Storybook's respect for continuity.

WHITEHALL LANE WINERY

Ocher and lavender, the colors of a California sunset, soften the geometric lines of Whitehall Lane, an angular, contemporary structure that stands in contrast to the pastoral setting of the vineyard. As if to telegraph the business at hand, the building's large windows have been cut in the shape of wine goblets. In front of the winery, a single row of square pillars runs alongside a walkway, each pillar supporting a vine that has entwined itself in the overhanging pergola.

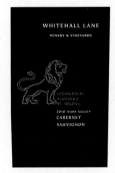

Glass doors open into a tasting room with a white beamed ceiling, cream walls with black-and-white photos of the vineyard, black counters, and concrete bar tops. The handsome interior befits an estate where the first grapevines were planted in 1880. Even then, Napa Valley settlers were drawn to Rutherford's deep, loamy soils and sunny climate. A vestige of those days, a barn built for equipment storage, is still in use today.

In 1979 two brothers bought the twenty-six-acre vineyard and founded the winery they named after the road that runs along the south border of the property. They produced Merlot and Cabernet Sauvignon before selling the property nine years later. The Leonardini family of San Francisco took over the Whitehall Lane Estate in 1993. Tom Leonardini, already a wine aficionado, had been looking for property to purchase. He was aware of the winery's premium vineyard sources and some of its outstanding wines. Moreover, unlike his previous enterprises, the winery presented an opportunity to create a business that could involve his entire family.

Leonardini updated the winemaking and instituted a new barrel-aging program. He also replanted the estate vineyard in Merlot and Sauvignon Blanc and began acquiring additional grape sources. Whitehall Lane now owns six Napa Valley vineyards, a total of 150 acres on the valley floor: the Estate Vineyard, the Millennium MM Vineyard, the Bommarito Vineyard, the Leonardini Vineyard, the Fawn Park Vineyard, and the Oak Glen Vineyard. The various wines produced from these vineyards were rated among the top five in the world on three occasions by *Wine Spectator* magazine.

Whitehall Lane's new building contains a barrel room and a crush pad, as well as a second-floor VIP tasting room. The goal of the facility is not to increase overall production, but to focus on small lots of Cabernet Sauvignon produced from the St. Helena and Rutherford vineyards. As the winery approaches its thirty-eighth anniversary, the Leonardinis have many reasons to celebrate the success of their family business.

WHITEHALL LANE WINERY
1563 St. Helena Hwy. S.
St. Helena, CA 94574
800-963-9454
greatwine@
whitehalllane.com
whitehalllane.com

OWNERS: Leonardini family.

LOCATION: 2 miles south of St. Helena.

APPELLATION: Rutherford.

HOURS: 10 A.M.–5:30 P.M. daily.

TASTINGS: $15 for current releases; price varies for reserve selections. No reservations required. Seated tastings by appointment.

TOURS: By appointment.

THE WINES: Cabernet Sauvignon, Chardonnay, dessert wine, Merlot, Pinot Noir, Sauvignon Blanc.

SPECIALTIES: Estate Cabernet Sauvignon, Leonardini Vineyard Cabernet Sauvignon, Millennium MM Vineyard Cabernet Sauvignon.

WINEMAKER: Jason Moulton.

ANNUAL PRODUCTION: 45,000 cases.

OF SPECIAL NOTE: Limited-production Leonardini Family Selection wines available only at the winery.

NEARBY ATTRACTIONS: Bothe-Napa State Park (hiking, picnicking, horseback riding, swimming); Culinary Institute of America at Greystone (cooking demonstrations); Robert Louis Stevenson Museum (author memorabilia); Napa Valley Museum (winemaking displays, art exhibits).

YAO FAMILY WINES

YAO FAMILY WINES
929 Main St.
St. Helena, CA 94574
707-968-5874
concierge@yaofamilywines
.com
yaofamilywines.com

OWNER: Yao Ming.

LOCATION: Downtown St.
Helena, west side of Main
St., next to Gott's Roadside.

APPELLATION: Napa Valley.

HOURS: 10 A.M.–5 P.M. daily.

TASTINGS: Access, $35 for
3 wines; Reserve, $50 for
3 red wines; Library, $80
for vertical tasting of 3 red
wines from different vin-
tages. Reserve and library
wines paired with artisan
cheese and charcuterie
plate.

TOURS: None.

THE WINES: Cabernet
Sauvignon, Sauvignon
Blanc.

SPECIALTY: Yao Ming
Family Reserve Cabernet
Sauvignon.

WINEMAKER:
Tom Hinde.

ANNUAL PRODUCTION:
4,000 cases.

OF SPECIAL NOTE: Collection of Yao Ming NBA
and Olympics basketball
memorabilia on display.
Glass-art chandelier by Rey
Viquez, Los Angeles architect. Napa Crest Sauvignon
Blanc and pre-2012 library
Cabernet Sauvignon avail-
able only at tasting room.

NEARBY ATTRACTIONS:
Culinary Institute of
America at Greystone
(cooking demonstrations);
Bale Grist Mill State Historic Park (water-powered
mill circa 1846); Robert
Louis Stevenson Museum
(author memorabilia).

A few months before his 2016 induction into basketball's hall of fame, the former NBA star Yao Ming waxed poetic about the "music on the court" that mesmerized him as an adolescent in China. He recalled with joy "the songs players hear" when their shoes scrape the floor, the ball swooshes through the net, competitors' muscles make contact, and how "you can hear your heart beat." As the starting center of the Houston Rockets, the seven-foot-six Yao spent many postgame evenings at Texas-style steak houses, along the way developing a similar passion for collector-quality Napa Valley Cabernet Sauvignon—so much so the Shanghai-born superstar established a winery whose debut 2009 vintage was released in 2011, the year he retired as a pro player.

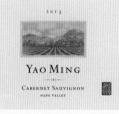

Wineries owned by cele-brities can be problematic affairs, but Yao assembled a top-notch team led by Tom Hinde, a respected winemaker whose experience ranges from smaller operations such as Flowers, a Chardonnay and Pinot Noir producer along the Sonoma Coast, to the megabrand Kendall-Jackson. For Yao Family Wines, Hinde focuses on Cabernet Sauvignon and other Bordeaux varietals under two labels, Yao Ming and Napa Crest.

The flagship wines are two Yao Ming Cabernet Sauvignons, one a reserve wine with grapes sourced from several Napa Valley subappellations. Aged the past few vintages in 100 percent new French oak for twenty-four months, the reserve consistently earns high scores from wine critics. The other Cab has been well received, too. You can imagine these wines with a steak or aged Gouda, but they're highly drinkable on their own. The accessible Napa Crest line includes a Sauvignon Blanc and a Cabernet-dominant proprietary red blend, both reasonably priced given the level of quality.

All tasting flights at Yao Family Wines, whose tasting room on downtown St. Helena's southern edge opened in 2016, include at least one of the flagship Cabernets. As with the other wines, these can be purchased by the glass as well. Though built for a previous tenant, the expansive space, with its large skylight, subdued shades of gray, up-lit quartz tasting bar, and art-installation chandelier made of two hundred China-red wine bottles, seems designed expressly for Yao.

The space provides a perfect showcase for the sports star's multifaceted interests. As promi-nent as the basketball memorabilia are photographs of the ex-player engaged in humanitarian projects that include educational outreach and the rescue and support of endangered rhinoceroses, elephants, and sharks. After tasting his wines and learning about his sports career and altruism, one gets the impression that the drive to excel with class and sensitivity is the unifying element.

ZD WINES

ZD WINES
8383 Silverado Trail
Napa, CA 94558
800-487-7757
zdwines.com

OWNERS: deLeuze family.

LOCATION: About 2.5 miles south of Zinfandel Ln.

APPELLATION: Rutherford.

HOURS: 10 A.M.–4 P.M. daily.

TASTINGS: UnWined seated tasting with selection of wines.

TOURS: By appointment. Eco Tour, Vineyard View Tour, Library Tour.

THE WINES: Cabernet Sauvignon, Chardonnay, Pinot Noir.

SPECIALTY: Abacus (solera-style blend of ZD Reserve Cabernet Sauvignon).

WINEMAKERS: Robert deLeuze, wine master; Chris Pisani, winemaker; Brandon deLeuze, associate winemaker.

ANNUAL PRODUCTION: 30,000 cases.

OF SPECIAL NOTE: Abacus tasting—comprehensive tour of cellar and tasting of reserve wines with a focus on Abacus.

NEARBY ATTRACTIONS: Bothe-Napa State Park (hiking, picnicking, horseback riding, swimming); Robert Louis Stevenson Museum (author memorabilia).

Driving along the Silverado Trail through the heart of Napa Valley, travelers are sure to notice ZD Wines. A two-ton boulder, from one of ZD's mountain vineyards, is adorned with the winery's striking gold logo, beckoning all to visit. A walkway lined with California native plants and grasses leads to the winery entrance. Inside the tasting room, a five-foot soil monolith showcases the Rutherford Estate Cabernet Sauvignon vineyard. Visitors find a cool respite on a hot summer day or a cozy place to linger in front of a fireplace in winter. Behind the tasting bar, large windows look into the ZD cellar, offering a glimpse of where the Chardonnay, Pinot Noir, and Cabernet Sauvignon they are sipping is crafted.

It has been said that winemaking isn't rocket science, but in fact, founding partner Norman deLeuze had been designing liquid  rocket engines for Aerojet-General in Sacramento when he met his partner Gino Zepponi. They decided to collaborate on producing classic Pinot Noir and Chardonnay and needed a name for their new enterprise. The aeronautical industry had a quality-control program with the initials ZD, referring to Zero Defects. This matched the partners' initials and created a new association for the letters ZD. In 1969 the winery purchased Pinot Noir grapes from the Winery Lake Vineyard in Carneros in southern Sonoma and produced its first wine, which was also the first wine ever labeled with the Carneros appellation. Soon after, the winery started making Chardonnay, ZD's flagship wine today.

Norman deLeuze turned to winemaking full-time, while his wife, Rosa Lee, handled sales and marketing. They purchased six acres, built their own winery, and planted Cabernet Sauvignon in Rutherford in 1979. Four years later, son Robert deLeuze was named winemaker. He had been working in ZD's cellars since he was twelve. In 2001 Robert passed the winemaking reins to Chris Pisani, who had worked closely with Robert for five years, building his appreciation and understanding of the family's consistent winemaking style.

Owned and operated by the deLeuzes for more than four decades, ZD Wines is a testament to the traditions, heritage, and passion of a true family business. Their success in crafting world-class wine has made them one of Napa Valley's iconic families. Founders Norman and Rosa Lee's two sons are currently at the helm of the winery: Robert deLeuze as CEO and wine master and Brett deLeuze as president. Grandchildren Brandon deLeuze and Jill deLeuze Billeci bring in the family's third generation, Brandon as associate winemaker and Jill in sales and hospitality.

SONOMA

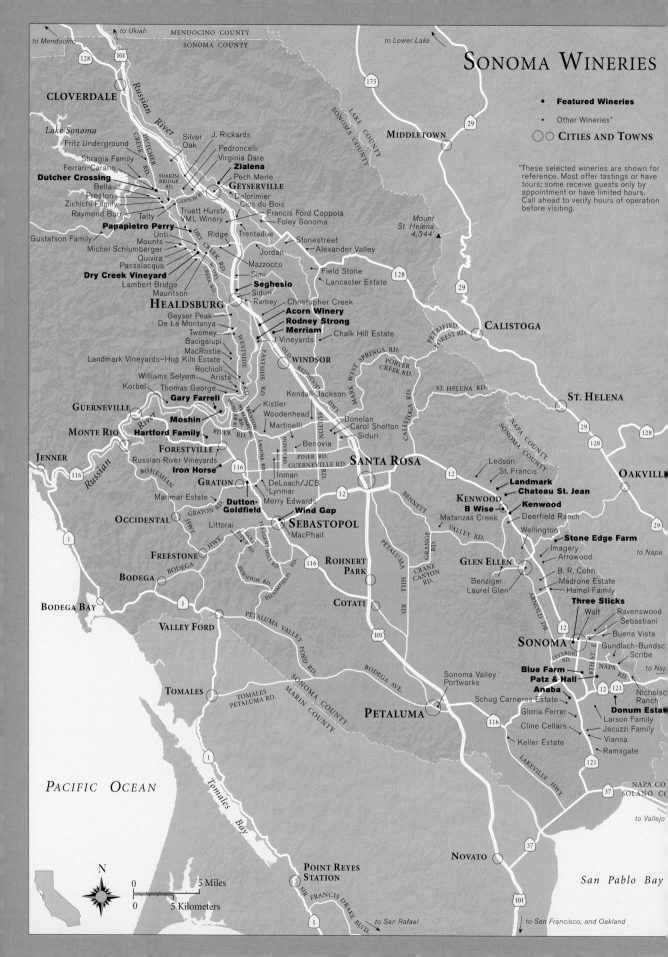

SONOMA WINERIES

- ● **Featured Wineries**
- • Other Wineries*
- ◯◯ CITIES AND TOWNS

*These selected wineries are shown for reference. Most offer tastings or have tours; some receive guests only by appointment or have limited hours. Call ahead to verify hours of operation before visiting.

MENDOCINO COUNTY
SONOMA COUNTY

to Mendocino
to Ukiah
to Lower Lake

CLOVERDALE

MIDDLETOWN

Russian River
Lake Sonoma

Fritz Underground
Silver Oak
J. Rickards
Pedroncelli
Virginia Dare
Zialena
Sbragia Family
Ferrari-Carano
Dutcher Crossing
Bella
Preston
Zichichi Family
Raymond Burr
Talty
Pech Merle
GEYSERVILLE
Delorimier
Clos du Bois
Truett Hurst/
VML Winery
Francis Ford Coppola
Foley Sonoma
Papapietro Perry
Unti
Ridge
Trentadue
Gustafson Family
Mounts
Michel Schlumberger
Jordan
Quivira
Passalacqua
Mazzocco
Dry Creek Vineyard
Simi
Lambert Bridge
Mauritson
Seghesio
Siduri
Ramey
Stonestreet
Alexander Valley
Field Stone
Lancaster Estate

Mount St. Helena 4,344'

CALISTOGA

HEALDSBURG
Geyser Peak
De La Montanya
Twomey
Bacigalupi
MacRostie
Landmark Vineyards~Hop Kiln Estate
Rochioli
Williams Selyem
Arista
Korbel
Thomas George
Gary Farrell
Christopher Creek
Acorn Winery
Rodney Strong
Merriam
J Vineyards
Chalk Hill Estate
WINDSOR
Kistler
Woodenhead
Martinelli
Kendall-Jackson
Donelan
Carol Shelton
Siduri

NAPA COUNTY
SONOMA COUNTY

ST. HELENA

GUERNEVILLE
Moshin
Hartford Family
MONTE RIO
FORESTVILLE
Russian River Vineyards
Iron Horse
GRATON
Marimar Estate
Dutton-Goldfield
Inman
DeLoach/JCB
Lynmar
Merry Edwards
Benovia
Wind Gap
SEBASTOPOL
MacPhail
SANTA ROSA
Ledson
St. Francis
Landmark
Chateau St. Jean
KENWOOD
B Wise
Kenwood
Deerfield Ranch
Matanzas Creek
Wellington
Stone Edge Farm
Imagery
Arrowood

JENNER

OCCIDENTAL
Littorai
ROHNERT PARK
GLEN ELLEN
B. R. Cohn
Madrone Estate
Hamel Family
Three Sticks
Walt
Ravenswood
Sebastiani
Benziger
Laurel Glen

FREESTONE
COTATI

BODEGA

BODEGA BAY

VALLEY FORD

Buena Vista
Gundlach-Bundschu
Scribe
SONOMA
Blue Farm
Patz & Hall
Anaba
Nicholson Ranch
Sonoma Valley Portworks
Schug Carneros Estate
Gloria Ferrer
Cline Cellars
Keller Estate
Donum Estate
Larson Family
Jacuzzi Family
Viansa
Ramsgate

TOMALES

PETALUMA

PACIFIC OCEAN

NOVATO

N

0   5 Miles
0   5 Kilometers

POINT REYES STATION

San Pablo Bay

to Napa
to Nap
to Nap
NAPA CO
SOLANO C
to Vallejo
to San Rafael
to San Francisco, and Oakland

OAKVILL
ST. HELENA

Sonoma boasts the greatest geographical diversity in California wine country. From the Pacific Coast to the inland valleys, to the Mayacamas Mountains that define the eastern border with Napa County, the countryside is crisscrossed by dozens of rural roads, making it an ideal destination for casual exploration.

Most of the county's oldest wineries can be found in the historic town of Sonoma. Facing the extensively landscaped eight-acre central plaza are nineteenth-century adobe and false-front buildings that now  house upscale shops, restaurants, and inns, as well as historic sites.

In the northern part of the county, the city of Healdsburg has recently evolved from a quiet backwater into the hottest destination in Sonoma County. It sits at the hub of three major grape-growing regions—Russian River Valley, Alexander Valley, and Dry Creek Valley—all within a ten-minute drive of the vibrant town plaza.

North of Santa Rosa, the Russian River Valley extends from the Healdsburg area almost all the way to the ocean, where the Sonoma Coast has become one of the most sought-after wine appellations. In addition to the colorful villages clustered along the coastal routes, the region offers boating, swimming, and fishing opportunities and the shade of giant redwoods that soar above the Russian River's banks.

ACORN WINERY

Here's a sleeper pick, a small winery with a historic vineyard whose down-to-earth owners, Betsy and Bill Nachbaur, chucked corporate jobs midcareer to pursue a passion for grape growing.

The couple purchased the twenty-six-acre vineyard in 1990 and renamed it Alegría, Spanish for "happiness." The grapes—chiefly Zinfandel dating as far back as 1890 but with numerous other varietals planted "field blend" style alongside them—were being sold in bulk. Within a year, Ridge Vineyard, a prominent California producer, was purchasing grapes from the Nachbaurs for a vineyard-designated Alegría wine. Noting the rich flavors the mix of grapes delivered, the tasting notes paid tribute to the "empirical wisdom of 19th-century growers." In the wake of this success and sales to other top wineries, ACORN was born, its name a nod to the property's many oaks, the oak barrels used to age the wines, and the adage that mighty oaks from the little acorn grow. These days, about a third of Alegría grapes are sold to other wineries, with the rest reserved for ACORN.

The Ridge Vineyard connection contained a touch of the poetic for Bill, whose early interest in field blending was piqued by his membership in Ridge's Advance Tasting Program. Members received shipments of single-vineyard wines, most of them old-school field blends made from varietals grown and fermented together, as opposed to the modern practice of growing, fermenting, and aging the grapes separately and blending them late in the winemaking process. Bill, who took viticulture and related courses at a local community college and at UC Davis, likens the traditional process to the making of a stew, contrasting the flavors achieved by melding all the ingredients in one big pot to what happens when they're cooked separately and combined at the end.

Though field blending doesn't always yield memorable wines, in Bill's capable hands the results are intricate and consistently balanced. Amid the Chardonnay- and Pinot-centric Russian River Valley, the ACORN lineup is refreshingly off the norm: Zinfandel (field blended with Alicante Bouschet, Petite Sirah, and other varietals), Syrah (plus a touch of Viognier), and Cabernet Franc (with Merlot and Petit Verdot) are the stars here, along with the Italian varietals Sangiovese and the relatively rare Dolcetto. Bill has the biggest challenge every year with the aptly named Medley, a blend of the sixty-plus varieties that flourish in Alegría.

Tastings, held in a modest space, are usually conducted by the Nachbaurs themselves, who often also venture into the vineyard with guests to explain their winemaking philosophy.

ACORN WINERY
12040 Old Redwood Hwy.
Healdsburg, CA 95448
707-433-6440
nachbaur@acornwinery
.com
acornwinery.com

OWNERS: Betsy and Bill Nachbaur.

LOCATION: 2.25 miles south of Healdsburg Plaza, about .5 mile off highway.

APPELLATION: Russian River Valley.

HOURS: 11 A.M.–4 P.M. daily, by appointment.

TASTINGS: $15 for 6 wines. Plate of local cheeses ($30) for two people with one-day notice.

TOURS: Vineyard tours available.

THE WINES: Cabernet Franc, Dolcetto, Sangiovese, Syrah, Zinfandel.

SPECIALTIES: Every wine a field blend of grapes of multiple varietals from certified sustainably farmed Alegría Vineyards, picked together and cofermented. Blends include Acorn Hill (Sangiovese, Syrah), Medley (60-plus grape types), Rosato (Rosé).

WINEMAKERS: Bill Nachbaur; Clay Mauritson, consulting winemaker.

ANNUAL PRODUCTION: About 3,000 cases.

OF SPECIAL NOTE: Winery is pet- and child-friendly. Casual ambience with picnic area. Owners often pour wines and lead vineyard walks. Oldest part of vineyard, planted in 1890, provides fruit for Heritage Vines Zinfandel.

NEARBY ATTRACTIONS: Lake Sonoma (boating, camping, hiking, swimming); Riverfront Regional Park (hiking, biking, kayaking, canoeing).

ANABA WINES

ANABA WINES
60 Bonneau Rd.
Sonoma, CA 95476
707-996-4188
inquiry@anabawines.com
anabawines.com

OWNERS: John and Kathleen Sweazey.

LOCATION: 4 miles south of the town of Sonoma at the intersection of Hwy. 121 and 116.

APPELLATION: Los Carneros.

HOURS: 10:30 A.M.–5:30 P.M. daily.

TASTINGS: $15 for 6 current-release wines.

TOURS: By appointment.

THE WINES: Chardonnay, Grenache, Mourvèdre, Petite Sirah, Picpoul Blanc, Pinot Noir, Port, Syrah, Viognier.

SPECIALTIES: Vineyard-designated Chardonnay and Pinot Noir, Rhône-style blends.

WINEMAKERS: Ross Cobb, Katy Wilson.

ANNUAL PRODUCTION: 7,500 cases.

OF SPECIAL NOTE: Tasting room located in a 100-year-old farmhouse. Tasting on a deck overlooking the vineyard. Wine available for purchase by the glass. Port-style wines, late-harvest Roussanne, and most vineyard-designated wines available only in tasting room.

NEARBY ATTRACTIONS: Mission San Francisco and other historic buildings in downtown Sonoma; Sonoma Raceway (NASCAR and other events); biplane flights; Cornerstone Sonoma (with *Sunset* test gardens and outdoor kitchen).

Tasters step into history when they visit the Anaba Wines tasting room in a farmhouse built a century ago. A simple structure, it features the high-pitched roof, front gable, and full-width porch typical of California's early rural construction. Fronted by two thirty-foot-tall Canary Island date palms—survivors of the original landscaping—it radiates a powerful sense of place. Nearby, a wind turbine cuts a striking figure against a backdrop of sky and the chaparral-streaked foothills of the Sonoma Mountains. Towering forty-five feet tall, it offers a clue to the meaning of the winery's intriguing name. Anaba (pronounced "anna-bah") derives from the word *anabatic,* which means "moving upward" and perfectly describes the Carneros appella-

tion's climate-defining winds.

When cool breezes off San Pablo Bay, located ten miles south, meet warm mountain slopes inland, they drift upward. The swirling winds drive away fog in the morning and cool the vineyards in the afternoon, which enhances the ripening process. They also spin the turbine's blades, generating clean power for the winery. Owners John and Kathleen Sweazey have taken further steps to run a green operation by sustainably farming the estate vineyards beside the farmhouse. They source additional fruit from vineyards throughout Sonoma County. In each location they meticulously farm their designated blocks. As a result, Anaba boasts an eclectic array of exquisite, small-lot Burgundian and Rhône-style wines. For fans of dessert wines, there are white and red Port-style wines, fortified with spirits distilled from estate-grown grapes.

A Chicago native, John discovered wine as a student at Stanford, where he spent weekends exploring Napa and Sonoma counties. After graduating with an economics degree in 1967, he spent nine months in Europe and developed an affinity for the wines of France's Rhône and Burgundy regions. Back in San Francisco, he built a successful real estate finance company and even did a little home winemaking. In 2006 John and Kathleen bought the Carneros property, which included eight acres of vineyards, most of which they replanted to Chardonnay and aromatic whites. Two years later, the couple introduced the Anaba label. They lovingly restored the farmhouse, fashioning the front living area into a tasting room, and opened to the public in 2009.

The room's vintage brick fireplace, open-beam ceiling, and ceramic pitcher full of fresh flowers reinforce the impression of a comfortable country home. Double french doors open onto a spacious redwood deck, where staff often pour seated tastings. The sheltered deck overlooks a lawn bordered by tidy beds of mixed roses, lavender, and ornamental grasses. Beyond the beds grow Chardonnay vines, their leaves gently rustling in the region's signature anabatic breezes.

B WISE VINEYARDS

B WISE VINEYARDS
9077 Sonoma Hwy.
(Hwy. 12)
Kenwood, CA 95452
707-282-9169
bwisevineyards.com

OWNERS: Brion and
Ronda Wise.

LOCATION: 11 miles northwest of Sonoma, 12 miles
east of Santa Rosa.

APPELLATIONS: Moon
Mountain District Sonoma
County, Sonoma Valley,
Fort Ross–Seaview.

HOURS: 10:30 A.M.–5:30 P.M.
daily.

TASTINGS: Kenwood Tasting
Flight, $20 for 3 or 4 wines.
Brion Society Reserve
Flight, $25 for 3 or 4 wines.

TOURS: Winery and cave
tour by appointment only;
call or ask at tasting room.

THE WINES: Cabernet
Franc, Cabernet Sauvignon,
Chardonnay, Petite Sirah,
Pinot Noir, Syrah, Tannat,
Zinfandel.

SPECIALTIES: Cabernet
Sauvignon, Pinot Noir,
single-vineyard Cabernet
Sauvignon, Trios (Cabernet
blend), Wisdom Red Blend.

WINEMAKERS: Massimo
Monticelli and
Mark Herold.

ANNUAL PRODUCTION:
5,000 cases.

OF SPECIAL NOTE: Heart
of Sonoma Valley Open
House (November). Moon
Mountain District cave tour
and tasting by appointment.
Most wines available only at
tasting room.

NEARBY ATTRACTIONS:
Annadel State Park (hiking,
biking); Quarryhill
Botanical Garden (Asian
plant collection); Sugarloaf
Ridge State Park (hiking,
camping, horseback riding).

A red sculpture fashioned of wine-barrel hoops marks the tasting space of B Wise Vineyards, an accomplished producer of artisanal red wines. The decor—cowhide sofa and matching chairs, ceramic tile floor, and poured-concrete bar supported by rough-hewn eucalyptus beams—creates a comfortably chic setting for sipping the Cabernet Sauvignon, Pinot Noir, and other wines of fourth-generation winemaker Massimo Monticelli. Mark Herold, who made his reputation crafting the Napa Valley's Merus Cabernet and other cult wines, collaborates on the Cabernets with Monticelli, himself a veteran of the acclaimed Silver Oak Cellars.

The winery's lowercase "b wise" logo seems a whimsical admonition to behave intelligently, but it's also a play on vintner Brion Wise's name. Wise grew up on an apple farm in Yakima, Washington, long before that area was known for wine, though the family grew grapes for homemade bottlings. He became a chemical engineer, but memories of winemaking intensified into a yearning to own a vineyard. In 2002 Wise bought a hundred-acre parcel on the western slope of the Mayacamas Mountains.

Wise's land, within the Sonoma Valley's Moon Mountain District, sits adjacent to the historic Monte Rosso Vineyard, established in 1880. *Monte rosso* means "red mountain," in this case in recognition of the area's thin layer of red volcanic ash soil that delivers bold, mineral-driven flavors. Wine collectors covet the Brion Monte Rosso Cabernet from grapes Wise purchases from this vineyard. He planted his own vineyard, twenty-one acres total, mainly to Cabernet Sauvignon, Zinfandel, and Syrah, with smaller amounts of Merlot, Petit Verdot, and other varietals used in wines such as the reasonably priced Wisdom Red Blend of all five.

Given Wise's agricultural background, it should come as no surprise that farming is a passion. His extensive preparatory research included determining, for instance, which Cabernet Sauvignon clones would perform best in particular vineyard sections. The flavors of different clones, or variants, of the varietal provide Monticelli and Herold a broad palette when assembling their wines, which also benefit from recent innovations in crop management and fermentation and aging techniques.

Guests at the airy Kenwood space, designed by Brion's wife, Ronda, sample flights of three or four wines. Monticelli also makes a sophisticated Chardonnay from grapes grown in the coastal Fort Ross–Seaview appellation. He shows himself equally adept working with Pinot Noir, achieving a lush mouthfeel yet retaining the varietal's delicacy and floral aromatics. As with the other B Wise offerings, for all the agricultural and technical know-how, the lasting impression is of sheer artistry.

BLUE FARM

BLUE FARM
221 San Luis Rd.
Sonoma, CA 95476
707-721-6773
memberservices@
bluefarmwines.com
bluefarmwines.com

OWNERS: Anne Moller-Racke
and Tim Mott.

LOCATION: 3 miles south of
historic Sonoma Plaza, off
Hwy. 12.

APPELLATION: Los Carneros.

HOURS: 10 A.M.–3 P.M.
Monday–Friday, by
appointment with 24 hours
notice.

TASTINGS: $45 for 4 or 5
wines.

THE WINES: Chardonnay,
Pinot Noir.

SPECIALTIES: Single-vineyard
Chardonnay from two
estates and other acclaimed
vineyards. Pinot Noir
from four appellations in
Sonoma County.

WINEMAKERS: Anne
Moller-Racke, winegrower;
Kenneth Juhasz, winemaker.

ANNUAL PRODUCTION:
1,500 cases.

OF SPECIAL NOTE: Tastings
include vineyard walk,
weather permitting, and
take place in 19th-century
pump house with view
of pond and 7-acre Anna
Katherina Pinot Noir
vineyard.

NEARBY ATTRACTIONS:
Mission San Francisco
Solano and other historic
buildings in downtown
Sonoma; Sonoma Valley
Museum of Art (modern
and contemporary art);
biplane flights; Cornerstone
Sonoma (with *Sunset*
test gardens and outdoor
kitchen).

About three and a half miles south of Sonoma Plaza but a generation removed in spirit and tone, Blue Farm occupies thirteen tranquil acres east of Highway 12. Nondescript agricultural properties line the quarter-mile of San Luis Road that leads to the former horse ranch and circa 1880 Folk Victorian home that winery co-owner Anne Moller-Racke purchased in 1999, but it takes only a minute or two on this magical parcel to grasp what inspired her to relocate here. Doves, sparrows, red-tailed hawks, and more than a dozen other species fly overhead; dragonflies and butterflies flit among the reeds in the pond out back; and San Pablo Bay breezes animate trees that include a waterside willow and a craggy-trunked pepper tree as old as the farmhouse itself. A restored nineteenth-century pump house and the weather-beaten windmill water pump that towers over it and the farmhouse also catch the eye.

Pastoral beauty aside, two other details attracted Moller-Racke to this property. With nearly two decades of experience farming Los Carneros AVA Pinot Noir at the time, she was aware that the distinctive soils and climate in the Sonoma County portion of the appellation were well suited for the varietal—and that the grapes for the esteemed Saintsbury winery's reserve Pinot Noir grew in a vineyard close by. Shortly after buying the ranch, Moller-Racke, who serves as president and CEO of Donum Estate, a respected Carneros Pinot player she cofounded, planted seven acres of four carefully selected Pinot Noir clones that produce two wines bearing the vineyard's name, Anna Katherina. Among the other wines, all from Sonoma County, are a Chardonnay and a Pinot Noir from the highly regarded Gap's Crown Vineyard and a Pinot Noir from the Martinelli family's Zio Tony Ranch in the Russian River Valley.

Moller-Racke, who was born in Germany, places herself in the European tradition of vignerons—winegrowers who farm with the intention of producing high-quality wines—but with a modern twist: she practices what's come to be known as "precision farming," using high-tech equipment to monitor the health of her vines and indicate when to intervene with irrigation, which she likens to a car's gas pedal, and other tools.

Moller-Racke's enthusiasm for farming is among the topics discussed on brief vineyard tours that begin, a glass of Chardonnay in hand, with a walk through another of Blue Farm's many delights, a 150-species rose garden tended as meticulously as the grapevines nearby. Tastings, always private and individually hosted, continue inside the pump house, whose views include the pond and the vineyards beyond, a serene setting that recalls the Sonoma of earlier times.

CHATEAU ST. JEAN WINERY

With the dramatic profile of Sugarloaf Ridge as a backdrop, the exquisitely landscaped grounds at Chateau St. Jean Winery in Kenwood evoke the image of a grand country estate. The château itself dates to the 1920s, but it wasn't until 1973 that a family of Central Valley, California, growers of table grapes founded the winery. They named it after a favorite relative and, with tongue in cheek, placed a statue of "St. Jean" in the garden.

The winery building was constructed from the ground up to suit Chateau St. Jean's particular style of winemaking. The founders believed in the European practice of creating vineyard-designated wines, so they designed the  winery to accommodate numerous lots of grapes, which could be kept separate throughout the winemaking process. Wines from each special vineyard are also bottled and marketed separately, with the vineyard name on the label. The winery makes a dozen vineyard-designated wines from the Sonoma Valley, Alexander Valley, Russian River Valley, and Carneros appella- tions. The winery also produces other premium varietals and one famously successful blend, the flagship Cinq Cépages Cabernet Sauvignon.

Chateau St. Jean became the first Sonoma winery to be awarded the prestigious Wine of the Year award from *Wine Spectator* magazine for its 1996 Cinq Cépages, a blend of the five traditional Bordeaux varietals, including Cabernet Sauvignon, Cabernet Franc, and Malbec. The winery received high acclaim again when it was given the #2 Wine of the Year award from *Wine Spectator* for its 1999 Cinq Cépages Cabernet Sauvignon. Winemaker Margo Van Staaveren has more than thirty years of vineyard and winemaking experience with Chateau St. Jean, and her knowledge of Sonoma further underscores her excellence in highlighting the best of each vineyard.

In the summer of 2000, Chateau St. Jean opened the doors to its new Visitor Center and Gardens. A formal Mediterranean-style garden contains roses, herbs, and citrus trees planted in oversized terra-cotta urns arranged to create a number of open-air "rooms." Visitors have always been welcome to relax on the winery's redwood-studded grounds, but now the setting is enhanced by the extensive garden plantings and a bocce ball court.

Beyond the Mediterranean garden is the tasting room with a custom-made tasting bar. Fashioned from mahogany with ebony accents, the thirty-five-foot-long bar is topped with sheet zinc. The elegant château houses the Reserve Tasting Room. Visitors who would like to learn more about Chateau St. Jean wines are encouraged to make a reservation for a more in-depth program.

CHATEAU ST. JEAN WINERY
8555 Sonoma Hwy.
Kenwood, CA 95452
707-257-5784
chateaustjean.com

OWNER: Treasury Wine Estates.

LOCATION: 8 miles east of Santa Rosa.

APPELLATION: Sonoma Valley.

HOURS: 10 A.M.–5 P.M. daily, except major holidays.

TASTINGS: $15 in main Tasting Room; $25 in Reserve Tasting Room.

TOURS: None.

THE WINES: Cabernet Sauvignon, Chardonnay, Fumé Blanc, Gewürztraminer, Malbec, Merlot, Pinot Blanc, Pinot Noir, Riesling, Syrah, Viognier.

SPECIALTIES: Cinq Cépages and vineyard-designated wines.

WINEMAKER: Margo Van Staaveren.

ANNUAL PRODUCTION: 500,000 cases.

OF SPECIAL NOTE: Picnic tables in oak and redwood grove. Wine education classes. Store offering gourmet food and merchandise. Bocce ball court.

NEARBY ATTRACTION: Sugarloaf Ridge State Park (hiking, camping, horseback riding).

DONUM ESTATE

DONUM ESTATE
24520 Ramal Rd.
Sonoma, CA 95476
707-939-2290
info@thedonumestate
.com
thedonumestate.com

OWNER: Winside.

LOCATION: 7.25 miles
southeast of historic
Sonoma Plaza, off
Carneros Hwy. 121/12.

APPELLATIONS:
Los Carneros, Russian
River Valley, Anderson
Valley.

HOURS: Daily, by
appointment.

TASTINGS: $50 for 5 wines.

TOURS: Short tour of parts
of estate included with
tasting.

THE WINES: Chardonnay,
Pinot Noir.

SPECIALTY: Pinot Noir.

WINEMAKER: Dan Fishman.

ANNUAL PRODUCTION:
4,000 cases.

OF SPECIAL NOTE: World-
class collection of sculptures placed in vineyards
and elsewhere on property.
Remains of an old stage-
coach stop erected in 1870
on-site. Most wines available only at winery.

NEARBY ATTRACTION:
Sonoma Valley Museum of
Art (modern and contem-
porary art); Cornerstone
Sonoma (with *Sunset*
test gardens and outdoor
kitchen); di Rosa (indoor
and outdoor exhibits of
works by contemporary
Bay Area artists).

With terrain that gently, haphazardly ripples north from San Pablo Bay, the Carneros appellation has been likened to a magic carpet, a description guests gazing out from the new Donum Estate hospitality building will quickly find apt. The simple wood and glass structure, atop a knoll where once dairy cows grazed, faces westward, with tall windows opening up to views of neatly coiffed Pinot Noir vineyards and, beyond them, recently restored bay marshland, the southern Sonoma Valley, and finally the hills of the Coast Range. The land's texture and setting first captivated Anna Moller-Racke, Donum's president and winegrower, nearly three decades ago. As director of vineyard operations for the historic winery then known as Buena Vista Carneros Estate, she converted it from pasture to vineyard.

When Buena Vista changed ownership in 2001, Moller-Racke came into control of a two-hundred-acre parcel she renamed Donum Estate. The winery quickly established a reputation for intense, refined Pinot Noirs that deftly split the difference between the overly fruity "power Pinots" popular at the time and the less assertive exemplars of the varietal that preceded them. Two vineyards here, Donum and Lawler, contain seventy-one acres of mostly Pinot Noir grapes, with a section of Lawler devoted to Chardonnay. Donum also owns a smaller vineyard, Winside, in the Russian River Valley, with sixteen acres planted mostly to Pinot Noir, and has a long-term lease on a vineyard in Mendocino County's Anderson Valley. All the Donum wines come from estate-grown fruit.

Moller-Racke sold Donum to Danish investors in 2011 but still runs the winery. The change has been felt in two key areas: architecture and art. The hospitality home, opening in 2017, is part of an infrastructure upgrade that includes a new winery facility—Donum's first one on-site—set to be fully operational by the same year's harvest. The bright white structures were designed as ultramodern variations on the dairy-era buildings that formerly graced the property. Striking a bolder pose are numerous large-scale contemporary outdoor sculptures by high-profile artists. Ai Weiwei, a Chinese artist and political activist of international renown, created the largest installation.

Tastings, usually of a Chardonnay, followed by a few Pinot Noirs, include a tour past Pinot Noir vines, some of the art, and the stone remains of an 1870s stagecoach stop. With the bay so close by, birds of dozens of species fly overhead, especially during spring and fall migration, cruising with the same San Pablo breezes that mitigate the height-of-summer heat on the grapes, facilitating their evolution into what Moller-Racke justly describes as serious wines made to last.

DRY CREEK VINEYARD

Dry Creek Vineyard president Kim Stare Wallace is justifiably proud of the many "firsts" credited to the winery's founder, her father. David S. Stare established the Dry Creek Valley's first post-Prohibition winery in 1972, the same year he planted the valley's first Sauvignon Blanc grapes. Stare later initiated the valley's successful bid for status as a distinct wine appellation and first used the term "Old Vine Zinfandel" to describe wines from grapes grown in pre-Prohibition vineyards. Stare modeled his winery after a Loire Valley château. Now covered with Boston ivy and fronted by a lawn shaded by tall redwoods, a magnolia, and other trees, the winery and its small tasting room have retained a homey feel. Stare, the winemaker in the early years, received favorable press for his debut Fumé Blanc, a Loire-style Sauvignon Blanc that remains Dry Creek's flagship white.

Long before Stare intro-duced Sauvignon Blanc, the Dry Creek Valley derived its renown from Zinfandel, a fact the winery acknowledges with old- and new-vine bottlings. The Heritage Vines and Old Vine Zinfandels are widely distributed, but limited single-vineyard offerings such as Beeson Ranch, from iron-rich soils in the southern valley, and Spencer's Hill, from the gravelly, sustainably farmed Endeavour Vineyard in the north, can be tasted only at the winery.

The early 2000s saw responsibility for the winery shift to the second generation, Kim and her husband, Don Wallace, though Kim's participation dates back to childhood chores that included working the bottling line and shoveling tanks clean. In the early 1980s, she suggested the winery honor the family's passion for sailing by commissioning nautical-themed label artwork. The success of this ongoing initiative led to an association with the sport that culminated in Dry Creek being named the official wine of two legs of the 2016 Louis Vuitton America's Cup World Series.

The Wallaces' overarching goal during the past decade has been to refine the accomplishments of Kim's father's era. To that end, they have refocused production on Dry Creek Valley wines and have invested millions in vineyard and winery upgrades. The couple elevated the program of Cabernet Sauvignon and Bordeaux-style red blends by hiring Tim Bell, a winemaker with experience making such wines at major Napa and Sonoma valley wineries. Bell has contributed his expertise to improve the winemaking process, as well as vineyard farming practices.

Well before Bell's arrival, Don Wallace set the winery on a path of sustainable agriculture, a com-mitment showcased in the insectary garden of beneficial plants and flowers installed near the tasting room. Guests are invited to stroll the garden, which borders an old-style, untrellised Zinfandel vineyard.

DRY CREEK VINEYARD
3770 Lambert Bridge Rd.
Healdsburg, CA 95448
800-864-9463
dcv@drycreekvineyard.com
drycreekvineyard.com

OWNERS: Stare-Wallace family.

LOCATION: 5.25 miles northwest of Healdsburg Plaza, off Dry Creek Rd.

APPELLATION: Dry Creek Valley.

HOURS: 10:30 A.M.–5 P.M. daily in summer; 10:30 A.M. – 4:30 P.M. daily in winter.

TASTINGS: $15.

TOURS: Winery tour ($30), 11 A.M. and 1 P.M. weekdays, by appointment. Self-guided vineyard walk and insectary garden (free) daily.

THE WINES: Cabernet Sauvignon, Chardonnay, Dry Chenin Blanc, Fumé Blanc, Merlot, Sauvignon Blanc, Zinfandel.

SPECIALTIES: Bordeaux blends, single-vineyard Sauvignon Blanc, Zinfandel.

WINEMAKER: Tim Bell.

ANNUAL PRODUCTION: 100,000 cases.

OF SPECIAL NOTE: Family-owned, 100 percent certified sustainable winery and vineyard. Blending seminars on weekends by appointment. Bocce ball court available by appointment for groups up to 12. Picnic grounds. Late-harvest Sauvignon Blanc, Rosé, and exclusive single-vineyard wines available only in tasting room.

NEARBY ATTRACTIONS: Lake Sonoma (boating, hiking, camping, swimming); Healdsburg Museum and Historical Society; Hand Fan Museum (collection of antique fans).

DUTCHER CROSSING WINERY

DUTCHER CROSSING WINERY
8533 Dry Creek Rd.
Geyserville, CA 95441
707-431-2700
866-431-2711
info@dutchercrossing
winery.com
dutchercrossingwinery
.com

OWNER: Debra Mathy.

LOCATION: 8.5 miles west of
Dry Creek Valley exit off
U.S. 101 via Dry Creek Rd.

APPELLATION: Dry Creek
Valley.

HOURS: 11 A.M.–5 P.M.
daily.

TASTINGS: $10 for weekday
flight, $15 for weekend
flight. Wine-and-cheese
pairings by appointment.

TOURS: Vineyard tours by
appointment.

THE WINES: Cabernet
Sauvignon, Chardonnay,
Merlot, Petite Sirah, Port,
Sauvignon Blanc, Syrah,
Zinfandel.

SPECIALTY: Zinfandel.

WINEMAKERS:
Kerry Damskey,
Nick Briggs.

ANNUAL PRODUCTION:
9,000 cases.

OF SPECIAL NOTE: Picnic
tables (reservations for
parties of 6 or more) and
pétanque court. Select
wines sold only at tasting
room.

NEARBY ATTRACTION:
Lake Sonoma (swimming,
fishing, boating, hiking,
camping).

Dutcher Crossing Winery exemplifies the low-key ambience of Dry Creek Valley, an appellation sixteen miles long and at most two miles across that has been home to generations of grape growers and winemakers. Sited at a scenic junction of two creeks—Dry Creek and Dutcher Creek—the small winery has a quaint charm, and its architecture evokes the look of the farming community that first flourished here in the early 1900s. A wide breezeway between the tasting room and the winemaking building offers panoramic views of the valley's hillside beauty.

Purchased by Debra Mathy in 2007, Dutcher Crossing produces small-lot, vineyard-designated wines crafted by winemakers Kerry Damskey and Nick Briggs. In addition to the signature Cabernet Sauvignon–Syrah blend, they make several Dry Creek Valley Zinfandels, select Chardon- nays from the Alexander Valley, and Pinot Noir sourced from the Russian River Valley. With more than fifty combined years as wine- makers, Damskey and Briggs are firm proponents of blending. Dutcher Crossing's Cabernet Sauvignon–Syrah is the first wine of its kind in Dry Creek Valley.

Proprietor Mathy expressed her adventuresome side by planting an estate vineyard block in the Châteauneuf-du-Pape style: a selection of Rhône varieties such as Grenache, Syrah, Mourvèdre, Cinsault, and Counoise. Guests can sip their selections while overlooking this planting from the trellised picnic area, set amid colorful gardens. Views of the valley landscape are also visible through the tall windows in the spacious tasting room, where highlights include a vaulted beam ceiling, a polished limestone tasting bar, and wide hickory plank floors. At one end of the rectangular room, a cozy conversation area with comfortable seating faces a fireplace made from locally quarried stone and topped with a mantel fashioned from distressed railroad ties. A vintage bicycle, the icon chosen to grace the Dutcher Crossing wine label, is also on display. It is a replica of the 1892 Rudge crafted in the classic Penny Farthing style so that the front wheel is larger than the back.

Debra Mathy considers the bicycle a symbol of the timeless qualities of an artisan approach to life as well as to winemaking. As the last Christmas present she received from her late father, it also represents her journey to find Dutcher Crossing Winery. Mathy, an avid cyclist and lover of bicycles since childhood, spent ten years traveling with her father to discover the winery of their dreams. She can almost always be found during the day greeting visitors, with her golden lab, Dutchess, at her side. Their friendliness and enthusiasm reflect the culture and spirit of Dutcher Crossing.

DUTTON-GOLDFIELD WINERY

Dutton-Goldfield Winery was born in 1998, when longtime friends Steve Dutton and Dan Goldfield shook hands in a historic vineyard on the western edge of the Russian River Valley. In the early 1960s, many people considered this region too cool for growing premium wine grapes, but at the time, fourth-generation farmer Warren Dutton, Steve's father, aimed to prove otherwise. The Dutton family had grown pears, hops, apples, and other crops in the Santa Rosa area since the 1880s. Dutton had a hunch that the cool-climate western Russian River Valley held excellent grape-growing potential. He ignored the naysayers and in 1964, with his wife, Gail, purchased thirty-five acres just west of the tiny town of Graton, located northwest of Sebastopol. He built a home and planted Chardonnay vines, hoping they would thrive close to cool Pacific breezes.

The vineyard became a success, and Warren Dutton's experiment encouraged other pioneering growers to plant wine grapes in the area. Dutton Ranch gradually acquired additional land and today includes more than 1,100 acres of grapes and 200 acres of organically farmed apples. Steve Dutton, his brother, Joe, and their mother, Gail, collectively operate the family business. Steve oversees the original Chardonnay vineyard and more than sixty additional plots of Chardonnay, Pinot Noir, Syrah, and Zinfandel in the Russian River Valley, Green Valley, and Sonoma Coast appellations. Many respected wineries purchase Dutton Ranch grapes to produce much-lauded Chardonnay.

The 1998 handshake marked a promising venture for Dutton Ranch—the union of Steve Dutton's extensive grape-growing expertise with Dan Goldfield's experience in the winemaking business. After Goldfield graduated from Brandeis University, he headed to California to pursue a career as a research chemist. His passion for Burgundian wines outweighed his love of lab work, and he decided to switch careers. He earned a master's in enology from UC Davis in 1986, then worked at Napa Valley wineries and spent two years in Portugal learning on the job. He subsequently honed specialized skills in crafting Pinot Noir and Chardonnay as winemaker at Sonoma County's La Crema Winery and Hartford Court. When the opportunity arose to team up with Steve Dutton, Goldfield jumped at the chance to make single-vineyard-designated wines sourced from a wide range of vineyards.

The Dutton-Goldfield tasting room opened in 2010 at the gateway to the village of Graton, near the Duttons' historic Chardonnay vineyard. The classy but casual space has seating areas for tastings by appointment and a bar for walk-ins. Weather permitting, guests sample wines on an inviting patio.

DUTTON-GOLDFIELD WINERY
3100 Gravenstein Hwy.
North
Sebastopol, CA 95472
707-827-3600
info@duttongoldfield.com
duttongoldfield.com

OWNERS: Steve Dutton and Dan Goldfield.

LOCATION: Northwest corner of intersection of Hwy. 116 (Gravenstein Hwy.) and Graton Rd.

APPELLATION: Russian River Valley.

HOURS: 10 A.M.–4:30 P.M. daily.

TASTINGS: Walk-in tastings complimentary with wine purchase, otherwise $20. Seated tastings and groups of 6 or more by appointment.

TOURS: None.

THE WINES: Chardonnay, Gewürztraminer, Pinot Blanc, Pinot Noir, Syrah, Zinfandel.

SPECIALTIES: Single-vineyard-designated Pinot Noir and Chardonnay.

WINEMAKER: Dan Goldfield.

ANNUAL PRODUCTION: 12,000 cases.

OF SPECIAL NOTE: Enclosed patio with tables and chairs. Tasting options include Wine and Sushi Flight, Wine and Cheese Flight, and Beast and Pinot Flight, as well as Vineyard Personalities Exploration. Rotating displays of work by local artists.

NEARBY ATTRACTIONS: Russian River (swimming, canoeing, kayaking, rafting, fishing); Armstrong Woods State Natural Reserve (hiking, horseback riding).

GARY FARRELL VINEYARDS AND WINERY

GARY FARRELL VINEYARDS AND WINERY
10701 Westside Rd.
Healdsburg, CA 95448
707-473-2909
concierge@
garyfarrellwinery.com
garyfarrellwinery.com

FOUNDER: Gary Farrell.

LOCATION: 12 miles southwest of downtown Healdsburg, near Wohler Bridge.

APPELLATION: Russian River Valley.

HOURS: 10:30 A.M.– 4:30 P.M. daily.

TASTINGS: By appointment.

TOURS: By appointment.

THE WINES: Chardonnay, Pinot Noir, Rosé, Sauvignon Blanc, Zinfandel.

SPECIALTIES: Vineyard-designated Chardonnay and Pinot Noir.

WINEMAKER: Theresa Heredia.

ANNUAL PRODUCTION: 25,000 cases.

OF SPECIAL NOTE: Sweeping view of Russian River Valley. Limited-production wines available only at winery.

NEARBY ATTRACTIONS: Russian River (rafting, canoeing, kayaking, swimming, fishing); Armstrong Redwoods State Natural Reserve (hiking, horseback riding).

A sharp turn off Westside Road leads up a driveway that climbs four hundred feet in elevation past native live oaks, madrones, and towering redwoods to one of the Russian River Valley AVA's early success stories. On many summer mornings, this short journey from the Russian River's northern bank transports visitors above the fog that glides in from the Pacific, enveloping rows of Chardonnay and Pinot Noir grapes on both sides of the river. Valley views stretching south, east, and west from the Gary Farrell tasting spaces and broad terrace create an enchanting backdrop for enjoying small-production, single-vineyard wines from these varietals.

The winery's namesake 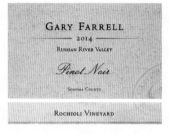 founder was among the first vintners to recognize the Russian River Valley's poten- tial for producing outstand- ing Chardonnay and Pinot. Farrell sold the winery more than a decade ago, but it still benefits from the relation- ships he established with renowned grape growers in Sonoma County and beyond. Theresa Heredia, a chemist turned winemaker known for taking calculated risks in harvesting, fermentation, and aging, crafts dynamic wines with grapes from Gap's Crown, Rochioli, Allen, Hallberg, Bacigalupi, and other storied vineyards. The soil types of these vineyards vary, but their climates are generally the same, with morning and late-afternoon Pacific breezes and fog tempering the midday summer heat. Such conditions result in a longer ripen- ing period, which helps the grapes develop richer flavors and attain proper acidity levels.

Heredia, who previously worked at Joseph Phelps Freestone Vineyards making Pinot Noir, likes to pick her grapes earlier than many of her Russian River Valley counterparts to avoid what she feels are the overly fruity characteristics that occur when berries are held too long on the vine. Her Pinots are vibrant yet reined in, her ideal Chardonnays "flinty, lemony, and savory," as she puts it. Though Pinot and Chardonnay are the winery's strong suits, the Zinfandels have always been noteworthy affairs. Under Heredia, working with this varietal for the first time, they are nuanced and lush.

Guests sample the impressive Gary Farrell lineup by appointment only at casually elegant seated tastings hosted by staffers well versed in the wines and the winery's lore. Given the consistency of both the climatic conditions and Heredia's winemaking style, a tasting here provides the opportunity to compare and contrast different vintages and vineyards and, particularly with the Pinot Noirs, the clones, or variants of the varietal. Subtly diverse, these wines are as beguiling as the setting itself.

HARTFORD FAMILY WINERY

Toyon, oak, and coast redwood fringe the sinuous country road that leads to the home of Hartford Family Winery. At the driveway, a one-lane bridge crosses Green Valley Creek into a forest clearing where the château-style winery offers a peaceful retreat. Sycamores shade the stately complex, and a fountain bubbles opposite the double doors of the tasting room. Furnished with European antiques, the spacious foyer opens into a space with crisp white cabinetry and a French limestone floor.

Renowned for crafting single-vineyard Chardonnay, Pinot Noir, and old-vine Zinfandel, the winery was founded in 1993 by Don and Jennifer Hartford. Don, whose family farmed strawberries in western Massachusetts, had re-cently concluded a successful law practice in Northern California and was drawn to the viticulture of Russian River Valley. With help from Jennifer's father, Jess Jackson, cofounder of Kendall-Jackson Wine Estates, the couple purchased the winery prop-erty about a dozen miles northwest of Santa Rosa.

Of the winery's fourteen Pinot Noir offerings, twelve are strikingly diverse single-vineyard bottlings made from 95 percent estate fruit. The estate vineyards thrive in five appellations: Los Carneros, Anderson Valley, Sonoma Coast, Russian River Valley, and Green Valley. All are cool-climate sites that yield small crops of often late-ripening grapes treasured for their flawless varietal flavors. The Far Coast Pinot Noir is sourced from estate vineyards located in Annapolis, on the Sonoma coast, some thirty miles north of the tasting room. For Chardonnay, the winery turns to the Sonoma Coast and Russian River Valley appellations. About 90 percent of the fruit is harvested from estate vineyards, including Fog Dance Vineyard, in the Green Valley AVA, and Seascape Vineyard, a six-acre ridgetop site facing Bodega Bay. The Hartfords craft five single-vineyard and one blended Zinfandel, all from dry-farmed Russian River Valley vines boasting an average age of a hundred-plus years. The grapes from these august vines exhibit rich berry and spice components born of both the vines' great age and the region's relatively chilly, protracted growing season.

The single-vineyard wines are made in limited lots, some as small as a hundred cases. During harvest, all the fruit is handpicked and then sorted by hand to remove everything but the best berries. Using only French oak barrels, the winemaker selects from nineteen different cooperages, matching barrels to each lot of wine to elevate the expression of both vineyard site and varietal characteristics.

HARTFORD FAMILY WINERY
8075 Martinelli Rd.
Forestville, CA 95436
707-887-8030
800-588-0234, ext. 1
info@hartfordwines.com
hartfordwines.com

OWNERS: Don and Jennifer Hartford.

LOCATION: 2 miles northwest of Forestville.

APPELLATION: Russian River Valley.

HOURS: 10 A.M.–4:30 P.M. daily.

TASTINGS: $15 for 6 wines. Private Library Tasting and boxed lunches available; reservations required.

TOURS: None.

THE WINES: Chardonnay, Pinot Noir, Port, Rosé, Syrah, Zinfandel.

SPECIALTIES: Single-vineyard Chardonnay, Pinot Noir, and old-vine Zinfandel.

WINEMAKER: Jeff Stewart.

ANNUAL PRODUCTION: 12,000–15,000 cases.

OF SPECIAL NOTE: Shaded picnic area with tables. Zinfandel Port and most single-vineyard wines available only in tasting room. Second tasting room located at 331 Healdsburg Ave., Healdsburg, open 10:30 A.M.–5 P.M. daily.

NEARBY ATTRACTIONS: Russian River (rafting, fishing, swimming, canoeing, kayaking); Armstrong Redwoods State Reserve (hiking, horseback riding); Laguna de Santa Rosa (freshwater wetlands with wildlife viewing).

IRON HORSE VINEYARDS

IRON HORSE VINEYARDS
9786 Ross Station Rd.
Sebastopol, CA 95472
707-887-1507
info@ironhorsevineyards
.com
ironhorsevineyards.com

OWNERS: Sterling family.

LOCATION: 7 miles northwest of downtown Sebastopol, off Hwy. 116.

APPELLATIONS: Green Valley of Russian River Valley, Sonoma County.

HOURS: 10 A.M.–4:30 P.M. daily. Friday–Sunday by appointment only.

TASTINGS: $25 for 5 wines (refunded with purchase).

TOURS: Tour and tasting ($30) weekdays 10 A.M.; Winemaker Truck Tour ($50) Monday 10 A.M.; both by appointment.

THE WINES: *Méthode champenoise* sparkling wines, Chardonnay, Pinot Noir.

SPECIALTIES: Special cuvées and single-vineyard-block Chardonnays and Pinot Noirs.

WINEMAKER: David Munksgard.

ANNUAL PRODUCTION: 24,500 cases.

OF SPECIAL NOTE: Oyster Sundays (April–October). Wood-slat picnic gazebo with vineyard view. Many of the wines available only at winery.

NEARBY ATTRACTIONS: Russian River (swimming, canoeing, kayaking, rafting, fishing); Armstrong Woods State Natural Reserve (hiking, horseback riding).

Tasting rooms at sparkling-wine houses tend toward the palatial, but with its open-air space, more Sonoma barn than château, the family-run Iron Horse Vineyards chose a more rustic approach. "Tasting the wines with a Pinot Noir vineyard spilling out at your feet feels magical," enthuses CEO Joy Anne Sterling. The close-up perspective on the surrounding hills duplicates the one that inspired her parents, Barry and Audrey Sterling, to acquire this land in 1976.

Half of Iron Horse's production is sparkling wines made from Pinot Noir and Chardonnay, with still wines from the same grapes comprising the other half. Today the winery is among the prominent producers in the Green Valley of Russian River Valley. Audrey Sterling spearheaded the creation of the appellation, but as with the winery's tasting space, settling here in the 1970s represented out-of-the-box thinking. Pinot Noir and Chardonnay were already being grown on the property, but not well, and the local agricultural agent advised them that the site was generally too cold and in spring too prone to frost. The Sterlings, who had lived in France and observed grapes thriving in cooler, rainier climes, begged to differ and took the plunge.

Four decades later, it's accepted wisdom that Green Valley, with its sandy-loam Goldridge soils, lingering morning fog, midday summer sunshine, and cool, foggy evenings, is prime Pinot and Chardonnay territory. On his engaging truck tours of the estate, winemaker David Munksgard describes the Sterlings as "visionaries with amazing instincts." He also credits advances in vineyard science, such as the strategy of "opening up the canopy" (pruning vines' leaves) to expose the grapes to more sunlight, with mitigating some of the factors that concerned the ag agent.

Iron Horse's big break came in 1985 when at a Cold War–era summit President Ronald Reagan and Mikhail Gorbachev of the Soviet Union toasted with the winery's Russian Cuvée, made especially for the occasion. Every administration since has served Iron Horse at state dinners at the White House, a public relations coup for the family. For a winery this size to have as many cuvées as Iron Horse does—*cuvée* refers to a special blend—is also unusual. "We've definitely got cuvée mania," jokes Joy Sterling of limited editions such as the seasonal Summer Cuvée, redolent of midyear stone fruit, and the slightly savory Winter Cuvée, and a Blanc de Blancs supporting oceanic conservation.

At tastings, guests can choose from all-bubbles flights or opt for all Chardonnay or Pinot Noir. If you find a bottle you like, you can picnic on the grounds and enjoy the dazzling view, which from the knoll on which the tasting room sits extends east on a clear day to the Napa Valley's Mount St. Helena.

KENWOOD VINEYARDS

A weathered redwood barn erected by Italian brothers John and Amandio Pagani in 1906 still catches the eye as visitors proceed along the driveway that leads to historic Kenwood Vineyards. When San Franciscan Mike Lee and three relatives bought the Pagani Bros. operation in 1970, it was the last pre-Prohibition winery in the small town of Kenwood still selling wine bearing its owners' name. The neighbors who'd remained in business were selling grapes or wine in bulk to Gallo and other large producers. At the renamed Kenwood Vineyards, Lee focused on making premium wines and within a few years had garnered a reputation for quality Cabernet Sauvignon, Zinfandel, and especially Sauvignon Blanc. Along with several other newcomer wineries, the group contributed significantly to Sonoma County's wine- making renaissance.

In 1976 Kenwood by contracting with the make an exclusive line of grapevines thriving in the writer's beloved Beauty tapped into literary history heirs of Jack London to wines from 130 acres of red volcanic soils of the Ranch in nearby Glen Ellen. The Jack London Vineyard wines—separate Cabernet Sauvignon, Merlot, Syrah, and Zinfandel bottlings bearing distinctive wolf labels—are still made today, with some of the proceeds used to support the adjacent 1,400-acre Jack London State Park, where the writer is buried.

Kenwood made history of its own by launching the highly praised Artist Series. Always crafted from the winery's best lots of Cabernet Sauvignon, the series has included label artwork by Charles Mingus III, Pablo Picasso, and Alexander Calder. The Artist Series got off to a controversial start with the 1975 vintage, whose label of a nude reclining on a vineyard hillside was rejected by the federal government for being "obscene and indecent." (The painting graced the 1994 vintage without incident.)

The current head winemaker, Pat Henderson, who got his start as an intern during the 1983 harvest and succeeded Lee in 2003, represents a link to Kenwood's roots. As Lee did, Henderson makes the wines cuvée style, with the grapes from each vineyard pressed (to release the juice), fermented, and aged separately to retain the lot's individual flavors. Based on those flavors, the winemaker determines the correct blend just before bottling. Until completion of a new tasting room scheduled to open in 2017, tastings will continue to take place where they have for decades, inside the humble, concrete-floored barn that got things rolling for the Pagani brothers a century ago.

KENWOOD VINEYARDS
9592 Sonoma Hwy.
(Hwy. 12)
Kenwood, CA 95452
707-282-4228
info@kenwoodvineyards
.com
kenwoodvineyards.com

OWNER:
Pernod Ricard USA.

LOCATION: 11 miles north of downtown Sonoma, 13 miles east of Santa Rosa.

APPELLATIONS: Alexander Valley, Dry Creek Valley, Russian River Valley, Sonoma Coast, Sonoma Mountain, Sonoma Valley.

HOURS: 10 A.M.–5 P.M. daily.

TASTINGS: Classic Tasting, $15 for 5 wines. Vintner's Choice, $25 for 5 wines.

TOURS: None.

THE WINES: Cabernet Sauvignon, Chardonnay, Merlot, Pinot Gris, Pinot Noir, Sauvignon Blanc, Syrah.

SPECIALTIES: Artist Series Cabernet Sauvignon; wines from Sonoma County appellations; various single-vineyard wines from author Jack London's former estate.

WINEMAKER: Pat Henderson.

ANNUAL PRODUCTION: 650,000 cases.

OF SPECIAL NOTE: Wines reflect diversity of Sonoma County climates and terrain. Picnic area. Many small-lot wines available only in tasting room.

NEARBY ATTRACTIONS: Annadel State Park (hiking, biking); Quarryhill Botanical Garden (Asian plant collection); Sugarloaf Ridge State Park (hiking, camping, horseback riding).

LANDMARK VINEYARDS

LANDMARK VINEYARDS
101 Adobe Canyon Rd.
Kenwood, CA 95452
707-833-0053
info@landmarkwine.com
landmarkwine.com

OWNERS: Stewart and Lynda Resnick.

LOCATION: Off Hwy. 12, 12 miles north of historic Sonoma Plaza.

APPELLATIONS: Los Carneros, Russian River Valley, Santa Lucia Highlands, Santa Maria Valley, Sta. Rita Hills, Sonoma Coast, Sonoma Valley, Monterey County, San Benito County.

HOURS: 10 A.M.–5 P.M. daily.

TASTINGS: $10 for 5 wines; $20 for single-vineyard wines.

TOURS: Estate Tour & Tasting ($30), 11 A.M. and 2 P.M., daily, by appointment. Horse Drawn Carriage Tour (free), May–September, Saturday noon–3 P.M.

THE WINES: Chardonnay, Pinot Noir.

SPECIALTIES: Small-production vineyard-designated wines.

WINEMAKER: Greg Stach.

ANNUAL PRODUCTION: 35,000 cases.

OF SPECIAL NOTE: Courtyard area for picnics and tasting. Bocce ball court. Private Tower Tastings ($40) of reserve wine in tower with 360-degree view. Annual events include Half Shells & Chardonnay Festival (May); Pig, Pizza & Pinot Festival (July); Harvest Festival (October). Many vineyard-designated wines available only in tasting room. On-site guest suite and cottage. Second tasting room featuring Landmark wines located at historic Hop Kiln winery.

This longtime local favorite sits along busy Highway 12 in Kenwood, but visitors often remark that its hacienda-style facility has the feel of a secluded vacation home. Valley oaks and poplars shade the landscaped outdoor courtyard, which faces eastward away from the highway toward Sugarloaf Ridge, the Mayacamas Mountains landform that dominates this section of northern Sonoma Valley. Especially on weekends, when the sounds of guests picnicking or playing cornhole and bocce ball fill the air, the place takes on a festive mood, but any day of the week this is a fine spot to enjoy Chardonnays and Pinot Noirs poured by knowledgeable, enthusiastic staffers.

Roses, wisteria, purple and white star jasmine, and other flowering plants provide seasonal splashes of color in the courtyard, with a large pond, a tall aquamarine fountain, and the nearby ridge the focal points. Following the winery's 1989 relocation here from nearby Windsor, many guests assumed that Sugarloaf repre-sented the titular landmark, but the name preceded the move. For the current owners, the name reflects their commitment to producing wines from landmark California vineyards, among them Sangiacomo, Rayhill, and Rodgers Creek in Sonoma County; Escolle Road in Monterey County; and Bien Nacido in Santa Barbara County.

Landmark's successful quest for quality grapes can be experienced up and down its lineup in leisurely tastings either in the courtyard or in the tall-ceilinged, Mexican-tiled indoor space. Overlook Chardonnay, the company's flagship wine, often scores well in blind tastings against pricier offerings, though given its stellar Sonoma County sources this isn't all that surprising. Winemaker Greg Stach displays an appropriately light touch with the several other Chardonnays, allowing the specific vineyard characteristics—the minerality of Sonoma Coast's Flocchini, for example, or the fruitier tendencies of Sangiacomo and Bien Nacido—to find expression in the wines. Stach shows equal finesse crafting the Pinot Noirs, whose stars include two midprice entrants, Santa Lucia Highlands (Monterey County) and Grand Detour (Sonoma Coast), along with the single-vineyard Rayhill (Russian River Valley) and Escolle Road (Santa Lucia Highlands) wines.

In 2016 Landmark took title on a bona fide landmark, the old Hop Kiln winery in Healdsburg. Built by Italian stonemasons in 1905 for use drying beer hops, the structure is considered the finest of its type still extant. Grapes for some of the Russian River's most noteworthy Chardonnays and Pinot Noirs are grown along Hop Kiln's stretch of Westside Road (trailblazing Rochioli is right next door), so Landmark's stature is only likely to increase as releases from these vineyards enter its portfolio.

"You can always replace the wine... but you can never replace the moment."
-Peter Merriam

MERRIAM VINEYARDS

MERRIAM VINEYARDS
11650 Los Amigos Rd.
Healdsburg, CA 95448
707-433-4032
info@merriamvineyards
.com
merriamvineyards.com

OWNERS: Peter and
Diana Merriam.

LOCATION: 3.5 miles south
of Healdsburg.

APPELLATION: Russian River
Valley.

HOURS: 10 A.M.–5 P.M. daily.

TASTINGS: Classic tasting
at bar, $15 (refunded with
wine purchase). Seated
tastings and tour for up
to 8, $35 per person, by
appointment.

TOURS: Complimentary
tours by appointment.

THE WINES: Cabernet Franc,
Cabernet Sauvignon,
Chardonnay, Merlot, Pinot
Noir, Rosé, Sauvignon
Blanc.

SPECIALTIES: Estate Pinot
Noirs, red Bordeaux
varietals.

WINEMAKER:
David Herzberg.

ANNUAL PRODUCTION:
3,000 cases.

OF SPECIAL NOTE: Library
wines available for pur-
chase. Picnic spot among
vineyards.

NEARBY ATTRACTION: Russian
River (swimming, canoeing,
kayaking, rafting, fishing).

When Peter and Diana Merriam wed in 1982, they honeymooned among the vineyards of France. The trip ignited a passion for wine, and in 1988 the New England natives bought a wine shop near Boston. They frequently traveled to France on business and to immerse themselves in the country's culture of food and wine. Eager to start a winery and promote the French style of living back home, the couple began searching for an established vineyard producing pedigreed fruit. Their quest culminated in 2000 in the purchase of the eleven-acre Windacre Vineyard. First planted to grapes in 1890, the vineyard, in the warmest corner of the Russian River Valley appellation, was replanted in 2003 with Cabernet Sauvignon and other Bordeaux varietals.

The Merriams blended California-style Bordeaux finding ideal acreage for mile east of the Russian secure permits and finish the winery and tasting year, the couple planted a Pinot Noir, Sauvignon Blanc, their first vintage of in 2000, three years before the winery about a half River. It took six years to construction, and in 2009 room opened. That same second estate vineyard to and Semillon on eight acres surrounding the winery. The vineyard was certified organic in 2011.

Despite the foray into Pinot Noir, Bordeaux-style red blends remain the focus. The common objective with all the wines, says winemaker David Herzberg, is to achieve a balance of tannins, acid level, fruit, and oak character, with each component elevating the finished product without calling attention to itself. To that end, the wines, some of whose fruit is purchased from carefully selected Sonoma County growers, are aged separately according to the vineyard or section where their grapes were grown. Throughout the aging process, Herzberg, a Healdsburg native, and Peter Merriam jointly make decisions about oak barrel types, toasting (briefly burning a barrel's interior to generate spicelike flavors), and the final blends.

Tastings at Merriam often begin with a glass of Sauvignon Blanc from grapes grown just outside the tasting room. The room and the winery stand on a low hill with views of rolling vineyards and coastal ridges to the west. Steeply pitched roofs and wide covered porches give the structures a New England flavor. Inside, the tasting room resembles a spacious farmhouse, complete with hand-hewn oak floors and an old table with a traditional soapstone top. In warm weather, some guests bring a picnic lunch and purchase a glass of wine to enjoy on the patio, an especially pleasurable experience as the afternoon progresses and the cooling Russian River breezes waft through.

MOSHIN VINEYARDS

MOSHIN VINEYARDS
10295 Westside Rd.
Healdsburg, CA 95448
707-433-5499
888-466-7446
moshin@moshinvineyards
.com
moshinvineyards.com

OWNERS: Rick Moshin
and family.

LOCATION: 10 miles southwest of Healdsburg.

APPELLATION: Russian River
Valley.

HOURS: 11 A.M.–4:30 P.M.
daily.

TASTINGS: $15 for 5 wines
(waived with purchase).

TOURS: By appointment
($30, includes tasting).

THE WINES: Chardonnay,
Merlot, Pinot Noir, Sauvignon Blanc, Zinfandel.

SPECIALTIES: Small-lot
vineyard-designated Pinot
Noirs, Perpetual Moshin
(Bordeaux blend), Moshin
Potion No. 11 (white
dessert wine).

WINEMAKER: Rick Moshin.

ANNUAL PRODUCTION:
9,000 cases.

OF SPECIAL NOTE: Russian
River Valley's only four-
tier gravity-flow winery.
Picnic area. Art gallery
with works by local and
other Northern California
artists. Events include
quilting show (winter) and
Barrel Tasting (March).
Most wines available only
in tasting room.

NEARBY ATTRACTIONS:
Armstrong Redwoods
State Natural Reserve
(hiking, horseback riding);
Russian River (rafting,
fishing, swimming,
canoeing, kayaking).

Westside Road out of downtown Healdsburg follows the mild curves of the Russian River past vineyards of mostly Chardonnay and Pinot Noir grapes. About ten miles southwest of town, both road and river bend sharply, and a colorful, far-larger-than-life sculpture of a hummingbird drawing nectar from a flower hovers in midair, marking the short, secluded driveway that ends at the Moshin Vineyards tasting room. Fronted by weathered redwood reclaimed from the century-old barn of a neighboring property, the room and the winery behind it nuzzle into the surrounding hillside so comfortably that it may come as a surprise to learn both were completed in 2005.

The winery and the wines

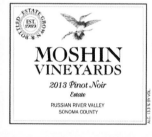

vision of Rick Moshin, a former for Pinot Noir wines is exceeded aspect of their creation. In this River Valley, it's not unheard of their tasting rooms to discuss

made within it represent the math professor whose passion only by his attention to every placid portion of the Russian for winemakers to appear in their wines with visitors, but

those lucky enough to stop here when Moshin is around might also hear him describe the intricacies of the energy-saving four-tier gravity-flow winery he designed, how he helped lay its foundation and build it, and how he milled and finished the sensually smooth tongue-and-groove black walnut tasting bar.

Sometimes a tasting bar is just a tasting bar, but in this case it provides clues about the artistry, precision, and scholarship that inform Moshin's lineup of a dozen-plus small-lot Pinot Noirs. They, along with Pinot Gris, Chardonnay, Zinfandel, and other wines, are made from grapes grown on twenty-eight estate acres and sourced from noted, mostly Sonoma County growers. Moshin, who started his winery in 1989, tends to pick Pinot Noir grapes on the early side to preserve the acidity, a European approach that often produces wines that pair well with food and age gracefully. They're also lower in alcohol than many of their Russian River counterparts.

Moshin's ultimate goal is to create affordable wines whose flavors—from the fruit, oak fermentation, tannins, and, most importantly, soil and climate—blend harmoniously. At tastings the choices include a few whites and, if available, a pale but zesty Rosé of Pinot Noir. The flavors of the Pinot Noirs range from the light and floral to bolder expressions of the varietal. The convivial, well-informed pourers share entertaining anecdotes about the wines, the winery, and the Russian River Valley appellation. The mood is so welcoming that in fine weather many guests extend their stay at the picnic tables near Rufus, the sculptural hummingbird, who's often joined by real ones flitting by.

PAPAPIETRO PERRY

A passion for Pinot Noir has connected Ben Papapietro and Bruce Perry for nearly forty years. Both grew up in San Francisco, in Italian and Portuguese families who always served wine at meals and gatherings. Their grandfathers made wine at home in the basement, and the young boys watched and listened, learning the basic techniques of the craft. They also developed a keen, lifelong interest in cooking and wine.

As a young man, Ben Papapietro sampled various Burgundian wines and fell in love with Pinot Noir. Purchasing this varietal for daily consumption, however, would certainly break the family bank. So he began making his own wines at home in the garage, following his ancestral tradi- tions. In the 1970s, while working at the San Francisco Newspaper Agency, he became friends with Bruce Perry, who sampled and liked Papapietro's garage-made wines and joined in on the endeavor. After producing several varietals, they knew it was Pinot Noir that won their hearts. Burt Williams, who worked at the San Francisco Newspaper Agency, was also an avid home winemaker. In the early 1980s,

Williams cofounded Williams Selyem, a Sonoma winery famed for its Pinot Noir production. Ben and Bruce worked there during annual harvests and honed their winemaking skills.

More than a decade later, the two friends felt ready to introduce their Pinot Noir to the public. They located a winemaking facility in Sonoma County and founded Papapietro Perry Winery in 1998. Bruce and Ben eventually left their day jobs and dove full force into the business, with Bruce and Ben making the wine and Bruce's wife, Renae, running the business. Later, Ben's wife, Yolanda, joined to handle distributor relations.

The devoted attention paid off quickly, as Papapietro Perry wines have consistently earned high praise and awards from critics since the early 2000s. Ben Papapietro's winemaking skills have also garnered acclaim among Pinot Noir devotees. Today the winery produces ten Pinot Noirs and a small amount of Zinfandel and Chardonnay. Grapes come from established vineyards in the Russian River Valley, as well as surrounding Dry Creek Valley, Anderson Valley, and the Sonoma Coast.

The Papapietro Perry tasting room opened in 2005 at Timber Crest Farms, in the heart of pastoral Dry Creek Valley. The former farm now houses a collection of wineries and other small businesses. Visitors taste wines at a gleaming copper-topped bar made of intricately woven barrel staves, which Bruce Perry built by hand. In many ways, the unpretentious space reflects the winery's homey, but humble beginnings in the family garage more than three decades past.

PAPAPIETRO PERRY
4791 Dry Creek Rd.
Healdsburg, CA 95448
877-GO-PINOT
707-433-0422
info@papapietro-perry
.com
papapietro-perry.com

OWNERS: Bruce and Renae Perry, Ben and Yolanda Papapietro.

LOCATION: 4.7 miles northwest of Healdsburg.

APPELLATIONS: Anderson Valley, Dry Creek Valley, Russian River Valley, Sonoma Coast.

HOURS: 11 A.M.–4:30 P.M. daily.

TASTINGS: $15 for 4 wines. Pinot on the Patio wine-and-cheese tasting by appointment.

TOURS: None.

THE WINES: Chardonnay, Pinot Noir, Rosé, Zinfandel.

SPECIALTY: Pinot Noir.

WINEMAKER:
Ben Papapietro.

ANNUAL PRODUCTION:
6,000–8,000 cases.

OF SPECIAL NOTE: Covered patio with tables and views of Dry Creek Valley; picnic area; bocce ball. Annual events include Winter Wineland (January), Barrel Tasting (March), Passport to Dry Creek Valley (April), Chardonnay and Lobster (June), and Wine and Food Affair (November).

NEARBY ATTRACTIONS: Lake Sonoma (hiking, fishing, boating, camping, swimming); Russian River (swimming, canoeing, kayaking, rafting, fishing); Healdsburg Museum and Historical Society (exhibits about Sonoma County); Hand Fan Museum (collection of antique fans).

PATZ & HALL

PATZ & HALL
21200 8th St. East
Sonoma, CA 95476
707-265-7700
info@patzhall.com
patzhall.com

OWNER: Ste. Michelle Wine Estates.

LOCATION: 3 miles southeast of historic Sonoma Plaza.

APPELLATIONS: Sonoma Valley, Sonoma Coast, Green Valley of Russian River Valley, Los Carneros, Russian River Valley, Mendocino.

HOURS: 10 A.M.–4 P.M. Thursday–Monday.

TASTINGS: $30 for 4 wines, held on the hour; $60 for Salon tasting of 6 reserve wines paired with food, by appointment.

TOURS: None.

THE WINES: Chardonnay, Pinot Noir, sparkling wine.

SPECIALTIES: Vineyard-designated Chardonnay and Pinot Noir.

WINEMAKER: James Hall.

ANNUAL PRODUCTION: 40,000 cases.

OF SPECIAL NOTE: Vineyard-view patio with seating, fountain, and large lawn with games. Gifts, jewelry, and wine-themed items available for purchase. Outdoor events monthly June–September. Annual events include Spring Release Open House (two Saturdays in March) and Fall Release Party (first Saturday in October). Many wines available only in tasting room.

NEARBY ATTRACTIONS: Historic buildings in downtown Sonoma; bike rentals; Vella Cheese Company.

Sonoma House, the gleaming new Patz & Hall hospitality center, sits amid lush vineyards in the rural east side of the town of Sonoma. For nearly a decade, the winery tasting room had been located in a modest office building near the city of Napa. When sixteen acres with a single-family residence became available up the road from its Sonoma winemaking facility, Patz & Hall seized the opportunity to transform the estate property into a one-of-a-kind wine country complex. The goal was to have a number of indoor and outdoor areas where the winery could welcome customers and get to know them in person. Sonoma House opened to the public in early 2014 following an extensive remodel that pre-  served the feel of a family home while adding contemporary flair and furnishings.

Patz & Hall was estab- lished in 1988 by four indivi- duals — Donald Patz, James Hall, Anne Moses, and Heather Patz — who dedicated them- selves to making benchmark wines sourced from distinctive California vineyards. Today, they produce a total of twenty Chardonnays and Pinot Noirs, all without owning a single vineyard themselves. Patz & Hall was founded on an unusual business model that began in the 1980s at Flora Springs Winery & Vineyards, when assistant winemaker James Hall and national sales manager Donald Patz forged a close friendship. Their mutual enthusiasm for wine produced from elite, small vineyards inspired them to blend their talents along with those of Anne Moses and Heather Patz. Together, the team boasted a wealth of knowledge and experience gleaned at such prestigious Northern California wineries as Far Niente, Girard Winery, and Honig Winery, where Hall was once the winemaker.

The founders applied their specialized expertise and daily attention to different areas of the winery's operations. The cornerstone of Patz & Hall is this integrated, hands-on approach, combined with close personal relationships with growers who supply them with fruit from outstanding family-owned vineyards.

Visitors to Sonoma House can sit on leather stools at the marble tasting bar, where casual tasting takes place, or can join a private, hour-long tasting, paired with food, in the elegant Sonoma House Salon. Guided tastings are also held on the shaded outdoor terrace. Over the course of an hour or more, guests sample single-vineyard wines paired with local farmstead cheeses and other light fare. Visitors are welcome to sink into comfortable sofas and chairs by a roaring fire in the living room in winter, or in fair weather in oversized rattan chairs on the terrace or back lawns, where they enjoy stunning views of the Mayacamas Mountains and estate vineyards.

RODNEY STRONG VINEYARDS

In the 1940s Rodney D. Strong trained with dance masters Martha Graham and George Balanchine at the American School of Ballet in New York. He enjoyed a successful career in the United States and abroad, including a four-year stint in Paris, where he developed a passion for food and fine wine. In 1959 Strong retired from dance, married his dance partner Charlotte Ann Winson, and planned to start a career in winemaking. The couple moved to Northern California, purchased a century-old boarding house in Sausalito, and began making their first wines.

As Strong perfected his winemaking skills, he proved to have an innate ability to see the potential of undiscovered growing regions. In 1962 he bought a turn-of-the-century winery and 159-acre vineyard in Windsor 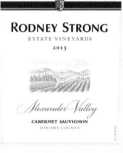 and replanted the vineyard to Chardonnay vines—the first in what later became the celebrated Chalk Hill AVA. In 1968, using U.C. Davis climate data as a guide, Strong purchased land in the Russian River Valley and planted several of the region's first Pinot Noir vineyards. He also built an impressive, efficient winery building, completed in 1970. Six years later, Rodney Strong Vineyards introduced Alexander's Crown, Sonoma County's first single-vineyard Cabernet Sauvignon. In 1977 the winery released the first Chardonnay bearing the Chalk Hill designation.

A decade later, as Strong was ready to transition into retirement, business consultant Tom Klein wanted to invest in the wine industry and recognized the untapped potential of Rodney Strong Vineyards. He convinced his family to purchase the winery in 1989. Over the decades, they installed state-of-the-art facilities, including a temperature-controlled barrel house and two artisan cellars for crafting small lots of wine. The family also took steps to reduce the winery's carbon footprint, and in 2009 Rodney Strong Vineyards became the first carbon-neutral winery in Sonoma County. Today it owns thirteen estate vineyards in six appellations, providing winemaker Rick Sayre, head winemaker since 1979, with a vast selection of varietals for crafting four tiers of wines: single vineyard, reserve, estate, and Sonoma County.

The original 1970 winery building continues to serve as the hospitality center, where visitors sample wines at a semicircular, granite-topped bar and at redwood-barrel tables. Exhibits on wine-making techniques and Sonoma County viticulture history are mounted along an open walkway and decks that surround the tasting room. On fair-weather days, seated food-and-wine pairings are held on the winery's canopy-shaded terrace, a new feature added in 2014, which is ringed with Chinese pistache trees.

RODNEY STRONG VINEYARDS
11455 Old Redwood Hwy.
Healdsburg, CA 95448
800-678-4763
info@rodneystrong.com
rodneystrong.com

OWNER: Tom Klein.

LOCATION: 3 miles south of Healdsburg via Old Redwood Hwy. exit off U.S. 101.

APPELLATIONS: Alexander Valley, Chalk Hill, Dry Creek Valley, Northern Sonoma, Russian River Valley, Sonoma Coast.

HOURS: 10 A.M.–5 P.M. daily.

TASTINGS: Complimentary for 2 wines; $10 for 4 estate wines; $15 for reserve tasting of 4 single-vineyard wines.

TOURS: Free guided tour at 11 A.M. and 3 P.M. daily. Self-guided tour 10 A.M.–5 P.M. daily.

THE WINES: Cabernet Sauvignon, Chardonnay, Merlot, Pinot Noir, Sauvignon Blanc, Symmetry (red Meritage Bordeaux blend), Syrah, Zinfandel.

SPECIALTY: Sonoma County vineyard-designated Cabernet Sauvignon.

WINEMAKERS: Rick Sayre, Justin Seidenfeld, Greg Morthole.

ANNUAL PRODUCTION: Unavailable.

OF SPECIAL NOTE: Summer outdoor concert series. Picnic area with tables on lawns overlooking vineyards. Extensive gift shop. Bar menu available in tasting room. Annual events include Winter Wineland (January), Barrel Tasting (March), Passport to Dry Creek Valley (April), and Wine and Food Affair (November).

NEARBY ATTRACTIONS: Russian River (swimming, canoeing, kayaking, rafting, fishing); Healdsburg Museum and Historical Society (exhibits about Sonoma County).

SEGHESIO FAMILY VINEYARDS

SEGHESIO FAMILY VINEYARDS
700 Grove St.
Healdsburg, CA 95448
707-433-3579
tastingroom@seghesio.com
seghesio.com

OWNER: Crimson Wine Group.

LOCATION: .75 mile north of Healdsburg Plaza, .5 mile south of Dry Creek Rd. exit on U.S. 101.

APPELLATIONS: Alexander Valley, Dry Creek Valley, Rockpile, Russian River Valley, Sonoma Valley.

HOURS: 10 A.M.–5 P.M. daily.

TASTINGS: $15 for 5 wines; $30 for 5 reserve wines, cheese, and house-made salumi. By appointment.

TOURS: By appointment.

THE WINES: Aglianico, Arneis, Barbera, Sangiovese, Vermentino, Zinfandel.

SPECIALTIES: Zinfandel and Italian varietals from Sonoma County; old vine and Home Ranch Zinfandels; Venom (Sangiovese).

WINEMAKER: Ted Seghesio.

ANNUAL PRODUCTION: 100,000 cases.

OF SPECIAL NOTE: Shaded picnic area, bocce ball court, terrace. Food-and-wine pairing ($75) Friday–Sunday by appointment. Special events include Passport to Dry Creek Valley (April); Zin and BBQ (July); Venom release party (October). Aglianico, Chianti Station Sangiovese, and small-lot Zinfandels available only in tasting room.

NEARBY ATTRACTIONS: Healdsburg Museum and Historical Society (changing exhibits about Sonoma County); Jimtown Store (country market, homemade foods).

A visit to this Healdsburg winery with a fascinating history would be essential even if its Zinfandel and other wines weren't so superbly crafted. The oldest estate vines date back to 1895, when Italian immigrant Edoardo Seghesio and his young wife, Angela, planted grapes at what's now known as Home Ranch. The couple purchased the Geyserville property using Edoardo's earnings from a decade of service at nearby Italian Swiss Colony, at the time California's largest wine producer. Edoardo owed more than his bankroll and grape-growing and winemaking knowledge to Italian Swiss. His boss, Angela's uncle, also played matchmaker, convincing Edoardo to delay a trip to Italy until she arrived from the old country. Introductions were made, the two hit it off, and the rest is northern Sonoma County history.

Before and long after Prohibition, the Seghesios, who established their winery in 1902, operated as bulk wine producers, over the years selling to Paul Masson, Gallo, and other large outfits. The family acquired the current location in 1949, but wines bearing the Seghesio label did not appear until 1983, when Edoardo and Angela's grandchildren and great-grandchildren, among them fourth-generation winemaker Ted Seghesio, who's still on the job, began crafting premium wines.

The winery's portfolio grew to include wines from more than two dozen varietals, but in recent years the focus has returned to Zinfandels and related blends from carefully selected Sonoma County vineyards. In a nod to the family's Italian heritage, Seghesio also makes Barbera and Sangiovese—the 1910 Home Ranch plantings of Sangiovese are thought to be North America's oldest—along with the relatively rare Arneis and Vermentino, two white varietals grown on an estate ranch in the nearby Russian River Valley appellation.

Seghesio's well-regarded Sonoma County Zinfandel accounts for three-quarters of production, and several other wines receive national distribution, but many of the small-lot Zinfandels, among them Pagani Ranch, from a vineyard first planted in the 1880s, are available only at the winery. The tasting room offers traditional stand-at-the-bar flights, and in fine weather guests can enjoy a flight—or a glass or a bottle—on the expansive front lawn. Staffers leading the popular food-and-wine pairings take guests on a guided tour before they sit down to bites prepared by executive chef Peter Janiak, and several times a year the dynamic duo of fourth- and fifth-generation vineyard managers Jim Neumiller and son Ned lead informative hikes through the Home Ranch vineyards up Rattlesnake Hill, a 40 percent slope whose terraced Zinfandel and Sangiovese vines are a sight to behold.

STONE EDGE FARM WINERY

A labor of joy and consummate teamwork, Stone Edge Farm is geared toward collectors of premium Cabernet Sauvignon. Private tastings take place at the winery's Silver Cloud Vineyard, 1,800 feet above the Sonoma Valley floor in the remote Moon Mountain District AVA. Silver Cloud lies down a narrow road that traverses the Mayacamas Mountains between Sonoma Valley's Glen Ellen and Oakville in the Napa Valley. Just getting here can be an adventure, but for most guests the transition to ease and relaxation commences before they enter the 160-acre property's 1920s farmhouse. Painted in muted green and gray, the home merges with the valley and coast live oaks, Japanese maples, and garden plants that surround it. This fetching tableau, viewed at most tastings from a salvaged-pine trestle living room, might enhance here the reverse happens: tricate Cabernets elevate Baker, who has been crafting these parts since the 1970s, for the intensity that its table in the home's former any well-made wine, but winemaker Jeff Baker's in- the experience substantially. sophisticated wines from extols Moon Mountain fruit volcanic ash soils impart.

Baker creates two estate-grown red wines each vintage, the Stone Edge Farm Cabernet Sauvignon and the Surround Red Bordeaux Blend. Most of the grapes for these balanced, complex wines come from Silver Cloud and Baker's Mount Pisgah Vineyard five miles away, with additional fruit from Stone Edge Vineyard, the valley-floor estate of winery owners John "Mac" McQuown and his wife, Leslie. The latter grapes, from the alluvial soils of the property's prehistoric riverbed, add velvety, almost voluptuous notes. Phil Coturri, dubbed the Wizard of Green by *Wine Spectator* magazine for his three-plus decades of organic agricultural practices, farms all three vineyards.

Stone Edge Farm's wines aren't distributed to shops or restaurant lists, with one exception: Edge, the winery's private dining room in downtown Sonoma. The extensive organic culinary garden at Stone Edge Vineyard supplies olive oil, fruit, herbs, honey, and more than 150 heirloom vegetables for the dishes of culinary director John McReynolds, whose credits include cofounding the popular Cafe La Haye across the street and a three-year stint as filmmaker George Lucas's executive chef.

A polymath and lifelong wine collector, Mac McQuown upended the financial-industry status quo nearly a half century ago when a Wells Fargo team he led developed the world's first stock index fund. He cofounded Monterey County's Chalone Wine Group and later collaborated with Baker on a different Moon Mountain project. Stone Edge Farm represents their mutual desire to produce world-class Bordeaux-style wines, showcased to discerning collectors in a casually luxurious setting.

STONE EDGE FARM ESTATE VINEYARDS & WINERY
P.O. Box 487
Sonoma, CA 95476
707-935-6520
info@stoneedgefarm.com
stoneedgefarm.com

OWNERS: Mac and Leslie McQuown.

LOCATION: 30-minute drive north of downtown Sonoma.

APPELLATIONS: Moon Mountain District, Sonoma Valley.

HOURS: Monday–Saturday, by appointment.

TASTINGS: $50 for 4 wines.

TOURS: Tastings include tour of winery, barn, gardens, and farmhouse.

THE WINES: Cabernet Sauvignon, Sauvignon Blanc.

SPECIALTIES: Estate-grown Cabernet Sauvignon from organically farmed vineyards.

WINEMAKER: Jeff Baker.

ANNUAL PRODUCTION: 3,500 cases.

OF SPECIAL NOTE: All wines available only through the winery. Edge, the winery's culinary home in downtown Sonoma, offers seasonal lunches, private dining, and culinary classes, by appointment. The award-winning *Stone Edge Farm Cookbook*, by Stone Edge culinary director John McReynolds, is available at all the winery's properties and on the winery's website.

NEARBY ATTRACTIONS: Jack London State Historic Park (hiking, historic sites, horseback tours); Quarryhill Botanical Garden (Asian plant collection).

THREE STICKS WINES

THREE STICKS WINES
143 W. Spain St.
Sonoma, CA 95476
707-996-3328, ext. 1
concierge@threestickswines
.com
threestickswines.com

OWNERS: Bill and Eva Price.

LOCATION: Half block west of
Sonoma Plaza's northwest
corner.

APPELLATIONS: Sonoma
Valley, Sonoma Coast,
Russian River Valley.

HOURS: 10:30 A.M.–4 P.M.
Monday–Saturday, by
appointment only.

TASTINGS: $35 for 4 current-
release wines, $70 for
7 library and current-
release wines.

TOURS: Guided tours of
historic Vallejo-Casteñada
Adobe included with tasting.

THE WINES: Chardonnay,
Pinot Noir.

SPECIALTIES: Small-lot, single-
vineyard Chardonnays and
Pinot Noirs.

WINEMAKER: Bob Cabral.

ANNUAL PRODUCTION:
5,000 cases.

OF SPECIAL NOTE: Adobe with
tasting salon is the oldest
occupied residence in
Sonoma. Original garden
designed by landscape
architect and gardening
writer and editor Helen
Van Pelt in 1948. Casteñada
Rhône blends available only
at winery.

NEARBY ATTRACTIONS:
Mission San Francisco
Solano and other historic
buildings in downtown
Sonoma; bike rentals; Vella
Cheese Company; Sonoma
Cheese Factory; Sonoma
Traintown (rides on a scale
railroad).

Bob Cabral, a renowned winemaker whose Pinot Noirs for the elite Williams Selyem Winery in Healdsburg often sold out upon and sometimes prior to release, created a buzz in early 2015 when he signed on with the smaller Three Sticks Winery. One attraction of the boutique operation for Cabral was the opportunity to make Chardonnays and Pinot Noirs, his specialties, from Durell and Gap's Crown, two legendary Sonoma Coast vineyards of the winery's owner, Bill Price. Cabral cited as another lure the chance "to get my hands purple again," focusing on artisanal winemaking instead of juggling the business side as well.

In addition to its estate vineyards, Three Sticks sources fruit for other Pinots and Chardonnays from equally noteworthy locales from Sonoma County grapes. the winery received high praise publications for the 2015 Char- under Cabral's control.

and makes a Cabernet Sauvignon Though best known for its Pinots, from *Wine Spectator* and other donnays, the first vintages entirely

The Three Sticks tasting salon is located steps west of Sonoma Plaza in an 1842 adobe, one of Sonoma's oldest structures. Following a painstaking restoration, Ken Fulk, a San Francisco– based celebrity designer, created an understatedly exuberant interior space that evokes California's period of Mexican rule (1822–1846) through its textures and earth tones, yet feels emphatically au courant.

The adobe's place in Sonoma history and the town's role in ushering in the modern era of California winemaking, which began a few miles away at Buena Vista Winery in 1857, are among the topics discussed at seated tastings limited to eight participants. The exclusive sessions, some of which involve locally sourced cuisine designed to pair with the wines, include a tour of the adobe and its garden, whose lush vegetation provides a backdrop for contemporary elements—fountains, a fire pit, and two arbors fashioned of willow branches supported by thick reclaimed Douglas fir beams. Depending on the weather and guests' preferences, tastings unfold either inside the adobe at a handcrafted elm table or outside in the garden at a cast stone one.

While Price was a principal in an investment company with wine holdings that included Chateau St. Jean in Kenwood, he developed a passion for Pinot Noir that eventually inspired the creation of Three Sticks. One might assume the origins of the winery's name are grape related, but they actually derive from his high school days in Hawaii as a surfer. His fellow surfers dubbed him "Billy Three Sticks," after the Roman numerals in his full name, Bill Price III.

WIND GAP WINES

Wind Gap bills its rustic-industrial space in the Barlow art, food, and wine complex in downtown Sebastopol as a tasting room and a wine bar, and with selections on tap for as little as $7 a glass, it has evolved into a mellow local hangout. Two story-tall garage doors create a welcoming atmosphere when retracted, and everything about the place, from the decor—heavy on concrete and unpainted reclaimed wood from Sonoma County barns and other old structures—to the soundtrack, which favors vinyl from 1980s and 1990s acts, says kick back, relax, and abandon preconceived notions about how wines should taste and wine tasting should unfold.

The tasting room's off-beat vibe sets the tone for wines like few others in all of Sonoma, some because they're crafted from rare grapes such as Trousseau Gris (back in the day known as Grey Riesling), others because winemaker Pax Mahle's techniques deviate so resolutely from the norm. With the Trousseau Gris, for instance, Mahle emphasizes the varietal's dusky minerality by fermenting the grapes largely in concrete, with some stainless steel, then introducing a pleasing roundness via a short stint in neutral French oak. Unlike many of his counterparts, with his red wines Mahle eschews new oak barrels in the aging process, opting instead for neutral (previously used) ones, always French, that impart fewer wood flavors. As with the whites, most of his reds spend time in concrete as well. Mahle coaxes an explosive fruitiness out of Grenache, Pinot Noir, and Syrah but without cloying sweetness.

Before entering the winemaking business, Mahle was a restaurant sommelier, a major influence on the way he approaches his craft. Wind Gap's wines bear several traits in common with others that critics have dubbed "New California Wines" to differentiate them from the jammy, "fruit-forward" products from the state that became popular beginning in the 1990s. These food-friendly wines are characterized by low alcohol and higher acidity, often the result of the grapes being grown in cool climates and picked earlier in the harvest cycle. The name of Mahle's winery acknowledges what many of the grape sources share: windy vineyards whose cool airflow slows ripening and heightens acidity.

A visit to Wind Gap, established in 2006, provides an easy opportunity to acquaint yourself with new trends in California winemaking. The Essential Flight, which includes one or more wines on tap, best illustrates the breadth of Mahle's oenological experimentations. You can also opt for a Classic Flight—two Chardonnays and two Pinot Noirs, one each from the Sonoma Coast and Santa Cruz AVAs—or a flight of Syrahs all from the Sonoma Coast. Whichever flight you choose, you're likely to find at least one of the wines you taste certifiably unique.

WIND GAP WINES
6780 McKinley St., Ste. 170
Sebastopol, CA 95472
707-331-1393
mail@windgapwines.com
windgapwines.com

OWNERS: Pamela and Pax Mahle, Charles and Ali Banks.

LOCATION: The Barlow, off Hwy. 12 in downtown Sebastopol.

APPELLATIONS: Mendocino, Russian River Valley, Santa Cruz Mountains, Sonoma Coast, Sonoma County.

HOURS: Noon–8 P.M. Friday and Saturday; 2 P.M.–6 P.M. Monday and Wednesday; noon–6 P.M. Thursday and Sunday.

TASTINGS: Wines available by the glass. Essential Flight, $16 for 4 wines; Classic or Syrah Flight, $25 for 4 wines.

TOURS: Upon request, time permitting; no charge.

THE WINES: Chardonnay, Grenache, Pinot Noir, Syrah, Trousseau Gris.

SPECIALTIES: Soif red blend of Valdiguie, Zinfandel, and several other old-vine grapes; wines on tap and sold by the growler.

WINEMAKER: Pax Mahle.

ANNUAL PRODUCTION: 10,000 cases.

OF SPECIAL NOTE: Winery is part of the Barlow, a 12.5-acre open-air community of artisan chefs; wine, beer, and spirits makers; and artists and craftspeople that opened in 2013 in a former apple-processing plant.

NEARBY ATTRACTIONS: Russian River (swimming, canoeing, kayaking, rafting, fishing); Armstrong Woods State Natural Reserve (hiking, horseback riding); Joe Rodota Trail (hiking and biking, partly along abandoned rail line).

ZIALENA

ZIALENA
21112 River Rd.
Geyserville, CA 95441
707-955-5992
info@zialena.com
zialena.com

OWNERS: Lisa and
Mark Mazzoni.

LOCATION: 1 mile northeast
of downtown Geyserville,
off Hwy. 128.

APPELLATION: Alexander
Valley.

HOURS: 10 A.M.–4:30 P.M.
daily.

TASTINGS: $15 for 4 wines;
$25 for 4 reserve wines.
Private tastings by
appointment.

TOURS: Grounds and winery
facility open for self-guided
tours.

THE WINES: Cabernet
Sauvignon, Chardonnay,
Sauvignon Blanc, Zinfandel.

SPECIALTIES: Cappella
(field blend); estate-grown
Cabernet and Zinfandel.

WINEMAKER: Mark Mazzoni.

ANNUAL PRODUCTION:
About 2,000 cases.

OF SPECIAL NOTE: Fourth-
generation grape-growing
and winemaking family,
three generations on this
site. Backyard gardens.
Pet-, bike-, and kid-friendly.
Guests welcome to picnic.

NEARBY ATTRACTIONS: Lake
Sonoma (swimming,
fishing, boating, hiking,
camping); Jimtown Store
(country market, home-
made foods).

A family affair four generations in the making, Zialena debuted in 2012, more than a century after Giuseppe Mazzoni, the great-grandfather of its proprietors, Lisa Mazzoni, and her brother, winemaker Mark Mazzoni, arrived in northern Sonoma County to work at Italian Swiss Colony. As did many Italian immigrants whose first stop was California's largest wine producer of the day, Giuseppe later became a grape farmer and winemaker himself.

The family ceased producing wine in the 1970s, but the third generation, led by Lisa and Mark's father, Mike, continued to farm. His company, Mazzoni Vineyards, supplies grapes to top wineries, most notably Jordan, which for more than a quarter century has purchased his fruit for its signature Cabernet Sauvignon. Mike, whose

120 acres of meticulous vineyards still stand prim and trim late in the season when some of their counterparts have begun to look tatty, sets aside for Zialena some of the same Cabernet grapes Jordan receives, along with Zinfandel Mark transforms into two wines. One is a reserve, justly praised for approaching the subtlety of its peers at Ridge Vineyards, the area's benchmark for the varietal. Mark has worked over the years on projects with Philippe Melka, one of the world's top winemakers and a proponent of complex, richly smooth reds. The influence of Mark's friend and mentor can be seen in the Cabernet, the Zinfandels, and the Cappella field blend.

Tastings at Zialena, which starting in 2017 take place at a new hospitality center set amid the family's vineyard, often begin with a Sauvignon Blanc that favors the varietal's citrusy characteristics, an admirably fresh Chardonnay, or both. Guests can opt for tastings that range from traditional stand-at-the-bar flights to library-style sessions in a private room whose windows open out to a secluded outdoor courtyard. Visitors can also purchase a glass or a bottle and relax on a patio surrounded by vines newly planted in the head-trained style that predominated during Giuseppe's era.

The treelike vines and their placement near the new tasting room represent a conscious attempt to link past and present. So, too, does the winery's name, which honors the oldest sister of Lisa and Mark's grandfather. Known in the family as Aunt Lena (*zia* means "aunt" in Italian), she embodied the warm-hearted hospitality Lisa wants to become the winery's trademark.

MENDOCINO

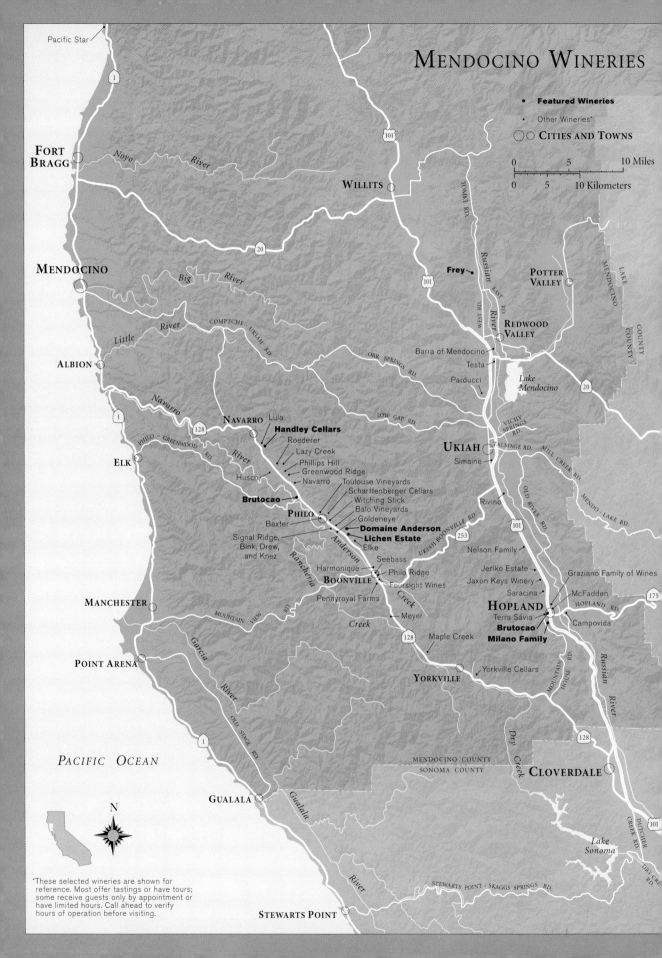

MENDOCINO WINERIES

- ● **Featured Wineries**
- · Other Wineries*
- ○○ **CITIES AND TOWNS**

0   5   10 Miles
0   5   10 Kilometers

Pacific Star

FORT BRAGG

WILLITS

Frey

POTTER VALLEY

MENDOCINO

REDWOOD VALLEY

Barra of Mendocino
Testa
Parducci

Lake Mendocino

ALBION

NAVARRO   Lula
Handley Cellars
Roederer
Lazy Creek
Phillips Hill
Greenwood Ridge
Husch   Navarro
Toulouse Vineyards
Scharffenberger Cellars
Witching Stick
Balo Vineyards
Brutocao   Goldeneye
PHILO
Baxter   **Domaine Anderson**
Lichen Estate
Signal Ridge,   Elke
Bink, Drew,   Seebass
and Knez   Harmonique   Philo Ridge
BOONVILLE   Foursight Wines
Pennyroyal Farms
Meyer
Maple Creek

ELK

UKIAH
Simaine
Rivino
Nelson Family
Jeriko Estate
Jaxon Keys Winery
Saracina
Graziano Family of Wines
McFadden
HOPLAND
Terra Sávia   Campovida
Brutocao
Milano Family

MANCHESTER

POINT ARENA

YORKVILLE
Yorkville Cellars

PACIFIC OCEAN

MENDOCINO COUNTY
SONOMA COUNTY

CLOVERDALE

GUALALA

Lake Sonoma

N

STEWARTS POINT

STEWARTS POINT - SKAGGS SPRINGS RD.

*These selected wineries are shown for reference. Most offer tastings or have tours; some receive guests only by appointment or have limited hours. Call ahead to verify hours of operation before visiting.

M endocino's dramatic coastline has made it famous all over the world, but the county offers a lot more than ocean views and rustic coastal inns. Now inland Mendocino is getting its due, thanks to local winemakers who are proving that their grapes are on a par with those of nearby Sonoma and Napa.

Vineyards were first planted here in the 1850s, when immigrants began farming food crops on the river plains and vineyards on the rugged hillsides and sun-exposed ridgetops. In time, they and their  successors found fertile ground in cooler areas that led them to achieve great success with a wide spec- trum of grape varieties. Located too far north to transport their wines to the San Francisco market by boat—as Napa and Sonoma winemakers could — Mendocino's early grape growers sold and traded their crops closer to home. In the 1960s, the wine boom and advances in shipping brought Mendocino wines to markets farther afield. Today, the county boasts more than a hundred wineries, so many of them involving organic wines or vineyards that the county bills itself as "America's Greenest Wine Region."

Mendocino's pioneer spirit still flourishes and is reflected in a serious respect for the environment. Most of the county is an undeveloped, pristine landscape offering abundant opportunities for enjoying an enviable variety of outdoor pursuits.

BRUTOCAO FAMILY VINEYARDS

Brutocao Family Vineyards is a tale of two families who combined their skills and expertise to establish one of Mendocino County's most notable wineries. The Brutocaos immigrated from Venice in the early 1900s, bringing with them a passion for wine. Len Brutocao met Marty Bliss while in school at Berkeley. Marty's father, Irv, had been farming land in Mendocino since the 1940s. Len and Marty married, and soon thereafter the families joined forces and began to grow grapes. The family sold their grapes to other wineries for years before starting to make their own wine in 1991. They selected the Lion of St. Mark from St. Mark's Cathedral in Venice as their symbol of family tradition and quality. The heart of that quality, they say, is in their 440 acres of vineyards in southern Mendocino County and another 11 acres of Pinot Noir in Anderson Valley.

Today, four generations of Brutocaos continue the family traditions, using estate grapes to produce a wide range of wines, including Italian varietals and blends. The wines are bottled under two labels: Brutocao Cellars, which focuses on premium vintages, and Bliss Family Vineyards, a new line of reasonably priced wines. The winery's first tasting room, a redwood building once occupied by another winery, is in Anderson Valley, site of the Brutocao family's eleven-acre cool-climate Pinot Noir vineyard. With its high-beamed ceilings, wisteria-covered patio, and umbrella-shaded picnic tables, it makes an ideal stop for those traveling scenic Highway 128 to the Pacific Coast.

In the late 1990s, the Brutocaos decided to open a second tasting room on U.S. 101. In 1997 they purchased the old Hopland High School from the Fetzer wine family and created a seven-and-a-half-acre complex, Schoolhouse Plaza, dedicated to food and wine. Both a tasting room and a banquet area with full kitchen are in the remodeled 1920s building, which still has its original facade bearing the high school's name. On display in the tasting room are memorabilia from the school's glory days. The complex also has a large conference room and an antique bar. Visitors can sip a glass of wine while perusing the large gift shop or overlooking the landscaped grounds, which include beautiful gardens of lavender, roses, and wildflowers.

The Brutocaos brought more than a love of food and wine when they came to this country. They are also passionate about bocce ball, a devilishly challenging game with a half-century Italian lineage. The Hopland complex has six regulation bocce ball courts, which are lighted and open to the public. Visitors can participate in friendly competitions free of charge or watch the games as they relax on terraces or the expanse of manicured lawn with a peaked-roof gazebo.

BRUTOCAO FAMILY VINEYARDS ANDERSON VALLEY TASTING ROOM:
7000 Hwy. 128
Philo, CA 95466
800-661-2103

SCHOOLHOUSE PLAZA:
13500 U.S. 101
Hopland, CA 95449
800-433-3689
brutocao@pacific.net
brutocaocellars.com

OWNERS: Brutocao family.

LOCATIONS: Hwy. 128 in Anderson Valley; U.S. 101 in downtown Hopland.

APPELLATIONS: Anderson Valley, Mendocino.

HOURS: 10 A.M.–5 P.M. daily (both locations).

TASTINGS: Complimentary.

TOURS: By appointment (complimentary).

THE WINES: Barbera, Cabernet Sauvignon, Chardonnay, Dolcetto, Merlot, Pinot Noir, Port, Primitivo, Sangiovese, Sauvignon Blanc, Zinfandel.

SPECIALTIES: Italian varietals, Quadriga (Italian varietal blend).

WINEMAKER: Hoss Milone.

ANNUAL PRODUCTION: 15,000 cases.

OF SPECIAL NOTE: Hopland: Bocce courts. On-site restaurant. Picnic areas with tables on shaded terraces. Annual events include Hopland Passport (May and October). Philo: Picnic area with tables and umbrellas under a shade arbor. Annual events include Anderson Valley Pinot Noir Festival (May). Port and reserve wines available only in tasting rooms.

NEARBY ATTRACTIONS: Hopland: Real Goods Solar Living Center (tours, store). Philo: Hendy Woods State Park (hiking, camping).

DOMAINE ANDERSON

DOMAINE ANDERSON
9201 Hwy. 128
Philo, CA 95466
707-895-3626
info@domaineanderson
.com
domaineanderson.com

OWNERS: Rouzaud family.

LOCATION: 5 miles
northwest of Boonville,
30 miles from Mendocino
coast via Hwy. 128.

APPELLATION:
Anderson Valley.

HOURS: 11 A.M.–5 P.M.
daily. (November–April
call for hours.)

TASTINGS: $8 (waived with
purchase of one bottle).

TOURS: By appointment.

THE WINES: Chardonnay,
Pinot Noir.

SPECIALTIES: Limited-
production single-
vineyard Chardonnay
and Pinot Noir.

WINEMAKER: Darrin Low.

ANNUAL PRODUCTION:
About 4,800 cases.

OF SPECIAL NOTE: Certified
biodynamic and organic
estate vineyards. Estate
honey, snack boxes,
and wine-themed gifts
available for purchase.
Shaded picnic tables on
veranda overlooking
vineyard. Winery is
dog-friendly. Anderson
Valley Pinot Festival open
house third weekend of
May; barrel tasting third
weekend of July; other
events throughout year.
Dach single-vineyard
Pinot Noir, Pinoli single-
vineyard Pinot Noir, Dach
Chardonnay, and Walraven
Chardonnay available only
in tasting room.

NEARBY ATTRACTIONS:
Hendy Woods State
Park (hiking, camping);
Navarro River (swimming,
fishing, wildlife viewing).

Famed French sparkling wine house Champagne Louis Roederer has been making classic European-style bottles of bubbly for nearly 250 years, and it is one of the last major Champagne houses to remain 100 percent family owned. In the early 1980s, Jean-Claude Rouzaud, a sixth-generation descendant of the founder, visited California to search for suitable land on which to establish a New World wine estate. In 1982 he discovered an ideal property at the northwest edge of the Anderson Valley and established Roederer Estate—now known as one of the top sparkling wine producers in the United States. The Rouzaud family's long-term plan was also to produce world-class still wines, especially Chardonnay and Pinot Noir from grapes grown in estate vineyards in the Anderson Valley AVA. In 2010 the Rouzauds seized an opportunity to purchase a vineyard and winery in the town of Philo. In 2011 they founded Domaine Anderson—the first time the family originated a winery in California devoted exclusively to still wines.

The meticulously tended certified organic vineyards are the heart of the Domaine Anderson winemaking program. All fruit is sourced from a total of fifty proprietary acres. Domaine Anderson wines are thus limited in production but demonstrate the impressive range of the Anderson Valley AVA's vineyard microclimates. The winery is able to combine Pinot Noir grapes from the three distinctly different growing areas within the Anderson Valley AVA—the cooler Deep End portion in the north, the warmer heart of the valley, and the even warmer Boonville region in the south. The seventeen-acre Dach vineyard that surrounds the winery facility and visitor center is certified biodynamic. All wines, predominantly Pinot Noir and a smaller amount of Chardonnay, are made in the Domaine Anderson facility, and famed French Burgundian winemaker Jeremy Seysses visits four times a year to consult with on-site winemaker Darrin Low, who previously crafted wine at J Vineyards, Grgich Hills Estate, and Flowers Vineyards.

The original winery building was designed in 2006 by renowned Bay Area architect Howard J. Backen, known for his simple, rustic, yet elegant style and use of natural materials. The stunning tasting room, completed in 2016, incorporates a similar urban-rustic style and elements that evoke the essence of Anderson Valley. Local artisans crafted many of the furnishings and decorative elements, including a thirteen-foot redwood table, and a bar, wainscot, and ledges made of VinoPlank, crafted from discarded toasted oak barrel inserts used in the fermentation process. Guests can also relax outdoors at shaded tables and seating areas overlooking the vineyards.

FREY VINEYARDS, LTD.

Arguably the most low-key winery in California, this gem is hidden off a two-lane road that wends through an undeveloped corner of Redwood Valley. Unsuspecting visitors might mistake the first building for the tasting room, but that's grandma's house. They must drive past it to reach the winery, and upon arriving, they find a charming little red house where tastings take place. Or when weather permits, tastings are conducted outdoors at a couple of planks set over a pair of wine barrels. Visitors are encouraged to picnic at one of several redwood tables and benches hand-hewn by the late family patriarch, Paul.

Virtually everything at  this winery seems handmade or fashioned from something else. Barrels and tanks have been salvaged from larger operations, and the winery itself was constructed of redwood from a defunct winery in Ukiah. Some rows of grapevines are interplanted with heirloom grains, which are harvested and ground into flour.

Frey (pronounced "fry") Vineyards is the oldest and largest all-organic winery in the United States. It may have another claim to fame as the winery with the most family members on the payroll. In 1961 Paul and Marguerite Frey, both doctors, bought ninety-nine acres near the headwaters of the Russian River. The Redwood Valley property seemed a great place to raise a family. Five of the couple's twelve children were born after the move, and most are still in the neighborhood.

In 1965 the Freys planted forty acres of Cabernet Sauvignon and Gray Riesling grapevines on the ranch's old pastureland, but they didn't start making wine until the 1970s. Eldest son Jonathan, who studied organic viticulture, began tending the vineyards and harvesting the grapes, which at first were sold to other wineries. When a Cabernet Sauvignon made with their grapes won a gold medal for a Santa Cruz winery, the family realized the vineyard's potential. Frey Vineyards was founded the next year, in 1980.

In 1996 the family began farming biodynamically. The word *biodynamic* stems from the agricultural theories of Austrian scientist and educator Rudolf Steiner. Biodynamic practices undertake to restore vitality to the soil. The farm is managed as a self-sustaining ecosystem, using special composting methods and specific planting times. As good stewards of the land, Frey started the first organic winery and was the first American winery fully certified by Demeter, the biodynamic certification organization. The wines have won many gold and silver medals for excellence.

FREY VINEYARDS, LTD.
14000 Tomki Rd.
Redwood Valley, CA 95470
707-485-5177
800-760-3739
info@freywine.com
freywine.com

OWNERS: Frey family.

LOCATION: 15 miles north of Ukiah off U.S. 101.

APPELLATION: Redwood Valley.

HOURS: 10 A.M.–4 P.M. Monday–Friday. Weekends by appointment.

TASTINGS: $10 (waived with purchase).

TOURS: 9 A.M.–5 P.M. Monday–Friday. Weekends by appointment.

THE WINES: Cabernet Sauvignon, Chardonnay, Merlot, Petite Sirah, Pinot Grigio, Pinot Noir, Sangiovese, Sauvignon Blanc, Syrah, Tannat, Zinfandel.

SPECIALTIES: Certified organic wines without added sulfites; biodynamic estate-bottled wines.

WINEMAKERS: Paul Frey and Jonathan Frey.

ANNUAL PRODUCTION: 200,000 cases.

OF SPECIAL NOTE: Picnic area for visitors' use. First American winery to receive Demeter biodynamic certification.

NEARBY ATTRACTIONS: Real Goods Solar Living Center (tours, store); Lake Mendocino (hiking, boating, fishing, camping); Grace Hudson Museum (Pomo Indian baskets, historical photographs, changing art exhibits).

HANDLEY CELLARS

HANDLEY CELLARS
3151 Hwy. 128
Philo, CA 95466
707-895-3876
800-733-3151
info@handleycellars.com
handleycellars.com

OWNER: Milla Handley.

LOCATION: 6 miles northwest
of Philo, 10 miles from
Mendocino coast.

APPELLATIONS: Anderson
Valley, Mendocino.

HOURS: 10 A.M.–6 P.M. daily
in summer, 10 A.M.–5 P.M.
daily in winter.

TASTINGS: Complimentary
for 5–9 wines; $15 for 5
reserve wines paired with
cheeses and estate products
such as olives and Pinot
Noir onion jam.

TOURS: By appointment.

THE WINES: Chardonnay,
Gewürztraminer, Pinot
Gris, Pinot Noir, red blends,
Riesling, Sauvignon Blanc,
Syrah, Zinfandel.

SPECIALTIES: Estate Chardonnay, Pinot Noir, sparkling
wine.

WINEMAKER: Randy Schock.

ANNUAL PRODUCTION:
8,500 cases.

OF SPECIAL NOTE: New picnic
area. Locally made jewelry
and international folk art
and crafts for sale in tasting room. Electric vehicle
charging station free for
guests. Events include Alsace
Festival (February), Pinot
Festival (May), and Anderson Valley Barrel Tasting
Weekend (July). Proprietary
blends, sparkling wine, and
late-harvest wines available
only in tasting room.

NEARBY ATTRACTION: Hendy
Woods State Park (hiking,
camping).

As the crow flies, Anderson Valley's "deep end"—the far western reaches of the AVA—lies just ten miles from the Pacific Coast. It's one of California's coolest grape-growing regions, where cool foggy nights and bright sunny days prevail, ideal conditions for Pinot Noir, Chardonnay, and Gewürztraminer cultivation. Handley Cellars occupies nearly sixty acres in the northwest corner of this pastoral region, accessible from east or west via scenic Highway 128. The estate was once part of the historic Holmes Ranch and still includes the original ranch house, barn, and water tower, built in 1908.

Owner and winemaker Milla Handley grew up in the Bay Area with cosmopolitan parents who made wine a regular part of the family meals. She earned a degree in fermentation science from UC Davis in 1975 and 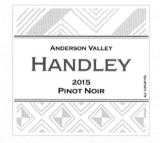 refined her craft working for winemakers Richard Arrowood at Chateau St. Jean and Jed Steele at Edmeades. In the early 1980s, eager to produce wine that reflected what she deemed the "essence" of Anderson Val-ley, Handley bought property at the Holmes Ranch. She planted her estate vineyard in 1982, built the winery three years later, and in 1987 opened the tasting room.

Handley shows her deep commitment to environmental stewardship in various ways. She farms responsibly, using organic methods and avoiding chemicals whenever possible. Behind the crush pad, she erected a solar array, which supplies 75 percent of the winery's energy. In 2013 she installed a complimentary electric vehicle charging station for environmentally conscious guests. To supplement the fruit grown in her thirty-acre vineyard—certified organic in 2005—Handley planted eight more acres at her home on the ridge above the winery. She also buys grapes from vineyards throughout Mendocino County, most from small family growers who share the same commitment to organic and sustainable farming. Handley crafts wines known for their distinctive character, balance, and ability to pair well with diverse international cuisines.

Handley Cellars rewards visitors with sweeping views of vineyard-stitched hills and ridgelines bristling with redwood trees—best enjoyed from shaded tables and Adirondack chairs in the new picnic area on the front lawn, completed in the summer of 2014. Indoors, the winery offers relaxed tastings amid a veritable gallery of antiques and folk art. When Handley was a child, her parents traveled to India, igniting a lifetime passion for collecting international folk art. Framed swatches of African Kuba cloth bear the angular patterns that inspired the winery's label art. In the adjacent courtyard garden, picnickers can enjoy a glass of wine while admiring antique sculptures.

LICHEN ESTATE

E very winter, the oak trees that speckle the hills and valleys of Anderson Valley lose their leaves, leaving ethereal drapes of green lichen hanging from otherwise bare branches. The graceful, lacelike organism appears everywhere in Mendocino County, from the Yorkville Highlands to the Mendocino coast—and Doug Stewart thus deemed Lichen Estate a fitting name for the 203-acre historic sheep farm in the heart of Anderson Valley that he purchased in 2000. The name also reflects the symbiotic relationship lichen has with its host trees, similar to the symbiosis winegrowers develop with the land.

Stewart and his wife, Ana Lucia Stewart, founded Breggo Cellars on the property in 2005. He bought fruit from various  renowned Anderson Valley vineyards and crafted his first vintage. Soon after, world-class accolades for Breggo wines started rolling in, and Breggo became one of the highest-rated wineries in Mendocino County history. In 2009 the Stewarts sold the Breggo brand but kept the land, with an eye toward starting a new venture focused on sparkling and still wines made from their own estate grapes. They planted seven acres of Pinot Noir and Pinot Gris in 2008 on meter-by-meter spacing (4,000 vines per acre), the same used for the Grand Cru vineyards of Burgundy and Champagne. Since the outset, they have farmed gently, meticulously, and organically. Creatures from sheep and honeybees to wild turkeys and deer live in harmony with the vineyard.

The first estate-grown wines were released at the end of 2013. Half of the harvest goes into the estate sparkling wine program and the other half to still wines: estate Pinot Noir and Pinot Gris. The sparkling wine Blanc de Noir is made with 100 percent Pinot Noir grapes, and the innovative Blanc de Gris entirely with Pinot Gris grapes. Grand Cuvée is the winery's *tête de cuvée*, the top bottling. It is 70 percent Pinot Noir and 30 percent Pinot Gris in most years. Creatively crafted still wines include the classic estate Pinot Noir; Solera, a multivintage blend of estate Pinot Noir grapes; Les Pinots Noir & Gris, an unorthodox blend of 60 percent Pinot Noir and 40 percent Pinot Gris grapes; and Moonglow, a combination of Lichen Estate and Anderson Valley Pinot Noir lots.

Lichen Estate's cozy, bungalow-style tasting room is in the heart of the Anderson Valley off Highway 128, its entrance marked by an inviting garden. Tastes are poured at a copper-fronted bar topped with reclaimed eucalyptus. Glass doors open out to the shaded porch and picnic tables, where guests can relax and take in sweeping views of redwoods and oak trees, decorated with lichen in every season.

LICHEN ESTATE
11001 County Rd. 151
Boonville, CA 95415
707-895-7949
info@lichenestate.com
lichenestate.com

OWNERS: Douglas Stewart and Ana Lucia Stewart.

LOCATION: About 3 miles north of Boonville, off Hwy. 128.

APPELLATIONS: Anderson Valley, Mendocino.

HOURS: 11 A.M.–5 P.M. daily.

TASTINGS: $5 for 3 or 4 wines. Reserve tasting $10 for 6 to 8 wines, by appointment. Barrel tasting $20, by appointment.

TOURS: By appointment.

THE WINES: Blanc de Gris and Blanc de Noir sparkling wines; Blanc des Noirs & Gris (white blend), Les Pinots Noir & Gris (Pinot Noir and Pinot Gris white blend), Pinot Noir, Solera (Pinot Noir blend).

SPECIALTIES: Estate sparkling wines; white Pinot Noir & Gris blend; Solera (multivintage Pinot Noir blend).

WINEMAKER: Douglas Stewart.

ANNUAL PRODUCTION: 2,000 cases.

OF SPECIAL NOTE: Shaded picnic tables on pet-friendly veranda. Solera (multivintage Pinot Noir blend) available only in tasting room.

NEARBY ATTRACTIONS: Hendy Woods State Park (hiking, camping); Navarro River (swimming, fishing, wildlife viewing).

MILANO FAMILY WINERY

MILANO FAMILY WINERY
14594 S. Hwy. 101
Hopland, CA 95449
707-744-1396
tastingroom@
milanowinery.com
milanowinery.com

OWNERS: Ted and Deanna
Starr.

LOCATION: .5 mile south of
Hopland.

APPELLATION: Mendocino.

HOURS: 10 A.M.–5 P.M. daily.

TASTINGS: $5–$8.

TOURS: By appointment.

THE WINES: Bordeaux
blends, Cabernet
Sauvignon, Carignane,
Charbono, Late Harvest
Cabernet, Late Harvest
Zinfandel, Malbec,
Merlot, Petit Verdot, Petite
Sirah, Port, Sangiovese,
Valdiguie, Zinfandel.

SPECIALTIES: Late-harvest
wines, Ports, and red
wines.

WINEMAKER:
Deanna Starr.

ANNUAL PRODUCTION:
2,500 cases.

OF SPECIAL NOTE: Most
wines available in tasting
room only. Wine-blending
seminar and barbecue
every June. Barrel Tasting
(last weekend in January).
Hopland Passport
Weekend (May and
October). RV parking.
Large, covered picnic area.
Tasting room sells wide
range of gift items. Dogs
welcome.

NEARBY ATTRACTION:
Real Goods Solar Living
Center (tours, store).

If history has a fragrance, it probably comes close to the woodsy aroma of the old hop kiln that houses Milano Family Winery. Built in 1947 by the son-in-law of Achilles Rosetti, who operated Hopland's first winery, the structure is among the last three hop kilns in Mendocino County, and is the only one that visitors can view by appointment. From the late 1800s through the mid-1900s, local farmers grew thousands of acres of hops, whose dried flowers lend flavor to beer. The aptly named town of Hopland, less than a mile north of the winery, underscores the former dominance of the crop.

In 2001 Deanna and Ted Starr acquired the property—which first produced wine in 1977 and is the oldest working winery in Hopland—and restored its original name, Milano. The couple came from Southern California, where Deanna had worked for more than twenty years as a registered nurse and manager in the medical field. With her background in chemistry, she felt confident that she could translate the couple's passion for wine into a vinicultural career. Ted, who designed software for medical applications, had developed a successful program to help winery owners manage their business, and was equally eager for a more rural way of life.

Set at the foot of Duncan's Peak, well back from a quiet stretch of Highway 101, the seven-acre parcel resembles a tidy farm, complete with a menagerie of animals. Sheep graze in a green pasture, roosters wander freely, and ducks flutter near a creek bed. There are pygmy goats, land tortoises, a llama, pot-bellied pigs, and, of course, dogs—the Labrador retriever Cuvee, the Labradoodle Star, and a sweet Pomeranian, Zeus.

Stepping up to the second-floor tasting room—where hops once cured on redwood slats—visitors can see the clear grain of the now-rare heart redwood from which the three-story structure was built. Tastings take place at a chest-high bar, and windows afford views of neighboring vineyards growing opposite the highway. A winemaker, but admittedly not a farmer, Deanna procures her fruit from a handful of dedicated growers, most of them in Mendocino County. The winery produces a wide variety of big reds, dessert wines, and quirky whites.

Visitors to Milano Family Winery who schedule a tour will likely find Deanna leading it, sharing her story with enthusiasm. She often stops to offer samples in the cool barrel room downstairs, where workers once bundled dried hops.

ACKNOWLEDGMENTS

Creativity, perseverance, integrity, and commitment are fundamental qualities
for guaranteeing the success of a project. The artistic and editorial teams who worked
on this edition possess these qualities in large measures. My heartfelt thanks go to
K. Reka Badger, Cheryl Crabtree, and Daniel Mangin, writers; Robert Holmes, photographer;
Judith Dunham, copyeditor; Linda Bouchard, proofreader;
Poulson Gluck Design, production; Scott Runcorn, color correction;
and Ben Pease, cartographer.

In addition, I am grateful for the invaluable counsel and encouragement
of Chester and Frances Arnold; Olivia Atherton; my esteemed parents,
Estelle Silberkleit and William Silberkleit; my wife, Lisa Silberkleit;
Danny Biederman; and the scores of readers and winery
enthusiasts who have contacted me over the past decade to say
how much they enjoy this book series.

I also extend my deepest appreciation to Taher Zaki and the staff of the
Hampton Inn in the town of Ukiah, California, for their excellent
hospitality and enthusiastic support of this project.

— Tom Silberkleit

OTHER BOOKS BY WINE HOUSE PRESS

The California Directory of Fine Wineries — Central Coast
Santa Barbara • San Luis Obispo • Paso Robles

Also available in e-book format for iPad, Kindle, Kobo, Nook, and other tablets.

Wine House Press
127 East Napa Street, Suite E, Sonoma, CA 95476
707-996-1741

Editor and publisher: Tom Silberkleit
Original design: Jennifer Barry Design
Production: Poulson Gluck Design
Copyeditor: Judith Dunham
Cartographer: Ben Pease
Color correction: Eviltron
Photo editing assistant: Frances Arnold
Proofreader: Linda Bouchard

All photographs by Robert Holmes, except the following:
page 32 and page 33, bottom left: Adrián Gregorutti; page 38, bottom left: Bryan Gray; page 42, bottom right: Illumin8 Creative;
page 43: Lisa Sze; page 50: Chad Keig; page 74, bottom right: Jason Tinacci; page 80: courtesy Sterling Vineyards; page 89, bottom left:
courtesy ZD Wines, bottom right: Bob McClenahan; page 108, bottom left, and page 109: Steven Rothfeld; page 117: LG Sterling;
page 121: Timothy Wilson; page 122: Carrie Moore; page 123, bottom left: Nancy Woods, bottom right: Carrie Moore; page 151:
Nathan Frey; page 152, bottom left: Jeanne Eliades, bottom right: Faith Echtermeyer; page 153: Tom Liden.

Front cover photograph: Somerston Estate, Napa Valley, CA
Back cover photographs: top left: Domaine Carneros; top right: Beringer Vineyards;
bottom left: B Cellars; bottom right: Robert Mondavi Winery.

Printed and bound in Singapore through Imago Sales (USA) Inc.
ISBN-13: 978-0-9853628-3-6

Eighth Edition

Distributed by Publishers Group West, 1700 Fourth Street, Berkeley, CA 94710, www.pgw.com

The publisher has made every effort to ensure the accuracy of the information contained in
The California Directory of Fine Wineries, but can accept no liability for any loss, injury, or inconvenience
sustained by any visitor as a result of any information or recommendation contained in this guide.
Travelers should always call ahead to confirm hours of operation, fees, and other highly variable information.

Always act responsibly when drinking alcoholic beverages by selecting a designated driver or prearranged transportation.

Customized Editions

Wine House Press will print custom editions of this volume for bulk purchase at your request. Personalized covers and
foil-stamped corporate logo imprints can be created in large quantities for special promotions or events, or as premiums.
For more information, contact Custom Imprints, Wine House Press, 127 E. Napa Street, Suite E, Sonoma, CA 95476; 707-996-1741.

Join the Facebook Fan Page: www.facebook.com/CaliforniaFineWineries
Follow us on Twitter: twitter.com/cafinewineries
Scan to visit our website: www.CaliforniaFineWineries.com